THE WAY

MEANINGFUL SPIRITUALITY FOR A MODERN WORLD

LARRY JORDAN

Published by CRESTONE PRESS LLC
Arlington, Texas USA

ISBN 979-8-218-01126-0

Library of Congress Control Number: 2023914753

Printed in the United States of America

Cover and interior formatting by KUHN Design Group | kuhndesigngroup.com

For more information, please visit www.larryjordanauthor.com

TO MY GRANDSONS:

Jase Orozco, Liam Jordan, and Noah Jordan

who taught their Papa how to love unconditionally

CONTENTS

To study the Way is to study the Self.
To study the Self is to forget the Self.
To forget the Self is to be enlightened by all things.
To be enlightened by all things is to remove
the barrier between Self and other.

DOGEN ZENJI

FOREWORD

by Jim Palmer

Many people who leave their religious background and belief-system experience a major episode of existential angst. All the epic questions about God, the universe, life's meaning and purpose, and the afterlife, previously anchored in the certainty of religion's answers, are swept away in one fell swoop.

Now what?

Reading Larry Jordan's book, *The Way: Meaningful Spirituality for a Modern World*, is a good place to start. Do not mistake the title, *The Way*, as an arrogant claim to absolute truth. The title rightfully identifies the fact that a broad spectrum of fields of knowledge and investigation has produced a unified understanding of ultimate reality, even if different language is used to describe it.

Sounds like a suitable place to lay a new foundation, right? Whether leaving religion and starting over, or seeking to expand or deepen one's spirituality, taking a deep dive into the greatest spiritual, philosophical, and scientific discoveries discussed in *The Way* is transformative.

For 25 years, I have been counseling people through their religious deconstruction, as well as recovery and healing from religious trauma and spiritual abuse. As a Spiritual Director I support countless people in the unfolding of their spiritual journey. I am often asked about books I would suggest. These days I find myself telling people

13

to read *The Way*. If you read only one book to guide your deconstruction and reconstruction process, this would be the one to read.

There are several aspects of *The Way* that set it apart and make it a valuable resource for your spiritual journey and process. There is a ring of authenticity and humility in Larry's writing. A lifetime of seeking, researching, learning, evolving, and living the spiritual truths he explores in this book, gives it gravitas that is unique.

The Way is not a heady, academic, pedantic exposition, but a plain-spoken and relatable work that is both entertaining and enlightening. Larry created some useful study questions for *The Way*, which invite the reader to engage and process the book's themes, considering your own spiritual journey. There is additionally a reading list at the book's end, that the reader will find useful.

As a resource for spiritual deconstruction and reconstruction, *The Way* invites the reader to explore a wide spectrum of essential and compelling areas, including:

- Western and Eastern worldviews
- Views on "God"
- Deconstruction of Christian theology
- Mystical experience
- Protestantism and Catholicism
- Eastern spirituality
- Nonduality
- The new physics
- Hard problem of consciousness
- Jungian psychology
- Jesus reimagined

The point of *The Way* is not to prescribe a new belief system, but to prompt the reader to reflect more deeply, challenge your current beliefs, consider new insights, and ask questions it might never have occurred to you to ask. Larry writes, "I hope that you see how the Eastern religions, the mystics, and the scientists suggest that everyone is related, and everything is connected. When you get that point, and when it changes you and your spiritual practice, then your belief system is secondary."

Larry's perspective is not solely related to individual liberation but includes connecting spirituality to the world as well as human and planetary suffering. He writes, "I have found that I live a better life when I live as if there is a Oneness, as if we are supposed to bring our understanding of the absolute world, which is Oneness, to our relative world, which can seem disconnected and divided."

As a Spiritual Director, I consider *The Way* by Larry Jordan the one foundational book I can recommend for men and women who are in the process of cultivating a deeper and more authentic spirituality. As the founder of The Center for Non-Religious Spirituality I have seen the impact of the spiritual support and guidance he offers others. You might say that *The Way* is the culmination of a lifetime of Larry's seeking, unlearning, learning, self-actualization, and enlightenment.

Thank you, Larry Jordan!

Jim Palmer

Introduction

ABOUT THE BOOK

This book is intended for general interest readers. It is a broad survey, not a deep study. My journey was a search for universal Truth, rather than the truth in a particular tradition, so I explored Eastern religions and Western religions, and I studied the mystics of many traditions and the luminaries of modern science.

The mystics seek experiential knowledge of God and metaphysics, just as the scientists seek experiential knowledge of the Universe and physics. Both the mystics and the scientists perceive a oneness or unity with God or the Universe, which can be difficult to reconcile with the Western religions, but easy to reconcile with the Eastern religions. Most Western religions are dualistic, and most Eastern religions are nondual.

In the West, many people believe that we are "apart from God," and the notion of separation and otherness can be traced back to the creation accounts in the Bible. In the West, many people believe that God is "up there" and we are "down here," that there was a cosmic rift between God and humans, and that Jesus was sent to reconcile this rift.

In the East, many people believe that we are "a part of God," and the notion of oneness and unity can be traced back to the emphasis on wholeness, not holiness. Many people believe that God is in every-one and everything, that the True Self (or no-self in Buddhism) is one with the Universe, that the egoic self can obscure the True Self, and that we become enlightened when we realize the True Self.

This book is an honest reporting of my findings, not an impassioned promotion of my beliefs, and my intent is to ask interesting questions and discuss provocative perspectives, not to promote or refute a particular philosophy or theology. At times, it may appear that the book takes a critical look at Christian doctrine, but this is a focus only because I was raised in that tradition.

This book is called *The Way*, which is what most religions, including Christianity, were called before the priests and theologians displaced the mystics and sages. In Spanish, the word for "way" is *camino*, like the well-known Camino de Santiago or the less well-known Camino de Crestone, which I completed in 2017.

The Camino de Crestone is an inter-spiritual pilgrimage in Crestone, Colorado, where pilgrims visit spiritual centers representing many spiritual traditions. The pilgrims participate in discussions and experiences at each of the centers. *The Way* is a journey, as well as a destination, and all journeys are both experiential and intellectual.

The Way will describe what author Aldous Huxley and others called the "perennial philosophy," which Huxley believed underlies all traditions. It assumes that there is a Godhead or ground behind the Universe, that this unity is immanent and transcendent, and that we can commune or merge with the Godhead or ground of being by transcending our egoic selves.

WHY THE BOOK WAS DIFFICULT TO WRITE

Politics and religion are the "third rails" of modern conversation. There is simply too much partisanship in both realms to facilitate civil discourse. It is uncomfortable when we see that our findings contradict our belief systems, but it is even more uncomfortable when others think that our findings violate their belief systems.

The Way is a work of reporting. There are not many original thoughts here, but there is a lot of reflection on the thoughts of others. Where I believed that it was helpful to attribute them, I mentioned the authors or the works, but instead of an exhaustive list of footnotes, I include some helpful Suggestions for Further Reading.

The book has two major sections, a Deconstruction and a Reconstruction. In the first section, Deconstruction, we discuss how my study of my own tradition led me to challenge some of my beliefs.

Some people who have not done the homework may feel that their beliefs are being challenged, too, but some deconstruction is necessary to "soften the soil" for the reconstruction that follows.

In the second section, Reconstruction, we review how my study of the Eastern religions, the mystics, and the scientists helped to reconstruct a belief system that makes sense in the modern world.

Throughout the book, there are several gray boxes, which are autobiographical, and these sections are loosely based on the four stages of life, as they are generally understood in India:

- *Brahmacharya* is the student stage.

- *Grihastha* is the householder stage.

- *Vanaprastha* is the forest dweller stage.

- *Sannyasa* is the renunciant stage.

Also, there are several white boxes, which are editorial, including 9/11, which marked the start of my journey, and 11/9, which marked the end of my journey. The Dark Night of the Soul and Comments and Responses sections are the hinges of the book, where the journey and the book reset. At the end, I include some helpful Suggestions for Study Questions.

In the process of deconstructing and reconstructing my beliefs, I came to understand God in new ways and to radically transform my politics and my religion, even my personality. My reconstructed belief system has changed me for the better.

ABOUT THE JOURNEY

Over the past 20 years, I embarked on a long and difficult spiritual journey, attempting to better understand myself, the world around me, and my place in the world. My search led me to deconstruct everything I thought I knew about God.

When I began my journey, I assumed that I would validate my conventional Christian beliefs, but the more I learned, the more I realized that I had never really understood my beliefs or where they originated.

I read about history, mythology, philosophy, psychology, and theology, to understand the origins of religion.

I read about Catholicism, Protestantism, and Orthodoxy, from the first century to the twenty-first century, to understand the origins of my own religion.

I read about Buddhism, Hinduism, Islam, Jainism, Judaism, and Taoism to understand other traditions and the similarities and differences between them.

I read the mystics and the wise people of all traditions, to understand spirituality (which is an awareness of something much greater than myself) as opposed to religion (which is a set of beliefs and practices).

I read the scientists, especially the quantum physicists, to explore how our emerging understanding of the physical world might produce a new understanding of the metaphysical world that may be the fundamental nature of reality.

As someone who reads the whole bookshelf, not just the whole book, I was determined to see how the pieces fit together. I read more than 1,000 books, and I felt a responsibility to share what I learned with my family and friends, as well as with other seekers who might not have the time to do this themselves.

WHY THE JOURNEY WAS
DIFFICULT TO UNDERTAKE

The Way is not well-traveled. Most people never question what they are taught, never challenge their native traditions, never examine other traditions, never explore their native worldviews, and never investigate other worldviews.

Many people assume that their religion is revealed by God and that their doctrines are absolute, authentic, original, rational, unchanging, and universal.

Many people assume that their religion is "right," that their fellow believers are "chosen" or "saved," that their scriptures are inerrant, or that their traditions are infallible.

Many people believe some things so strongly that they "know" them, but beliefs are opinions, not facts, and we never know as much as we think we know. Having read more than 1,000 books, I know so much less than I used to know.

Sometimes we think that we "know" because we believe our scriptures are inerrant or our traditions are infallible, but those, too, are beliefs or opinions, not facts.

Sometimes we think that we "know" because our scriptures or our traditions tell us so, but we might not know where our scriptures or traditions originated, or (more important) what they mean.

Sometimes we think that we "know" because we believe our parents and priests, but how many of them did the homework to know anything about God? How many of them were seeking universal Truth, rather than the truth in a particular tradition?

If we write down all that we "know" about God, we produce a blank piece of paper. We know nothing about God, including whether God exists. All theology is speculation.

Barbara Brown Taylor, an Episcopal priest, asks, "What does any of us mean when we say 'God'? We use the word as if it were made of steel instead of silk netting."

BREATHING NEW LIFE INTO OLD BONES

I wrote most of this book in Crestone, and I discussed the book with James O'Dea, an activist and mystic who formerly led Amnesty International in the United States.

As we were discussing my book, James pulled out *The Sufi Book of Life* by Neil Douglas-Klotz and asked me to pick a page at random. My page told of Ezekiel blowing new life into old bones:

> 1 The hand of the Lord came upon me, and he brought me out by the spirit of the Lord and set me down in the middle of a valley; it was full of bones. 2 He led me all around them; there were very many lying in the valley, and they were very dry. 3 He said to me, "Mortal, can these bones live?" I answered, "O Lord God, you know." 4 Then he said to me, "Prophesy to these bones, and say to them: O dry bones, hear the word of the Lord. 5 Thus says the Lord God to these bones: I will cause breath[a] to enter you, and you shall live. (Ezekiel 37:1-5)

"Your book is supposed to blow new life into old bones," James said earnestly.

9/11

On September 11, 2001, Islamic terrorists flew airplanes into the World Trade Center. The world was shocked. Who were these people, why did they do it, and what did they believe? I wondered whether Islam (or any religion) actually condoned the slaughter of innocent citizens, so I began to study Islam, in order to find out.

THE MUSLIMS

I read the Quran and researched the history of Islam. The word "Islam" means "submission to God," and the five pillars of Islam are the declaration of faith, charity, daily prayers, fasting, and pilgrimage. Although some fundamentalists misunderstand the religion and justify terrorism in its name, Islam is generally a peaceful religion, and Muslims are generally peaceful people.

Throughout history, Muslims have lived peaceably with Christians and Jews, who are called "people of the book," not "infidels." Muslims have not often forced others to convert. Although there has been violence between Christians and Muslims, like the Crusades and the Inquisition, most of these incidents were initiated by the Christians.

THE SUFIS

I was particularly intrigued by the Sufis or the "whirling dervishes," who are the mystics of Islam. Rumi, a Sufi mystic, is one of the best-selling poets in the United States. His poetry is erotic and ecstatic, and he expresses his love for God in romantic terms that are as ardent as the love between a man and a woman. Throughout his poetry and prose, Rumi emphasizes the oneness of being.

"Why aren't there any Christian mystics?" I asked. Of course, there are Christian mystics, but organized religion often views them as heretics. Many churches are skeptical if the mystic circumvents the church or contradicts church teaching.

Martin Luther believed that man should seek union with God through suffering, the "theology of the cross," rather than through mystical experience, the "theology of glory."

I came to see that Islam is not the problem; fundamentalism is the problem. All religions have fundamentalists, people who think that religion is literal, not metaphorical, and doctrinal, not transformational.

For me, what began as a narrow exploration of Islam became a broader exploration of my own spiritual life and my own Christian tradition.

Along the way, I met some interesting, wonderful people who were also seekers, and I realized that I had a lot in common with other seekers, regardless of their beliefs. Also, I met people from other traditions who were more Christ-like than many Christians.

PART 1

DECONSTRUCTION

UNLEARNING

In *The Red Book* by Carl Jung, the author asks Ammonius the Anchorite how he can read the Bible so many times without encountering monotony. The monk replies:

> A succession of words does not have only one meaning, but men strive to assign only a simple meaning to the sequence of words, in order to have an unambiguous language…. What you call "knowledge" is an attempt to impose something comprehensible on life…. The word becomes your God, since it protects you from the possibilities of interpretation…. I've spent many years with the process of unlearning. Have you ever unlearned anything?

Sometimes, family members and friends ask me, "What is there to unlearn?" because they believe (as I did) that Christianity was revealed by God and that its doctrines are absolute, authentic, original, rational, unchanging, and universal.

Many people accept what they were told by their parents and priests, without question, as I did for the first 40 years of my life. Before we can construct a theology that makes sense, consistent with the insights of the mystics and the scientists, we have to deconstruct what we were told.

LEARNING

When I began my spiritual journey, I assumed that Christianity was historical and that my search would confirm my conventional Christian beliefs. I began by studying the history of Christianity from its beginnings, and eventually I studied other traditions, too.

At first, I confined my inquiry to conventional sources, because there is a lot of speculation in the spiritual literature. There are a lot of books about angels, Aquarians, astral bodies, astrology, Atlanteans, and the like. Because I have no evidence for any of these things, I will not discuss any of them in this book.

As my questions multiplied, I was forced to consider other traditions and worldviews, because there is a lot of speculation in contemporary Christian theology, too:

> The Trinity? That was Tertullian, 300 years after Jesus' death.

> Original sin? That was Augustine, 400 years after Jesus' death.

> Substitutionary atonement? That was Anselm, 1,000 years after Jesus' death.

> Justification by faith? That was Martin Luther, 1,500 years after Jesus' death.

> Papal infallibility? That was Pope Pius IX, 1,800 years after Jesus' death.

How many of the 12 apostles preached the Trinity, the one God of three persons? None of them, because the Bible did not even exist, the Trinity is not even in the Bible, and the doctrine of the Trinity was not even invented yet.

There are a lot of books about the Trinity, original sin, substitutionary atonement, justification by faith, papal infallibility, and the like. Because I have no evidence for any of these things, I will not advocate for any of them in this book, but I will address them.

When some people read the book, they say, "This is interesting, if it is true." Fortunately, you do not have to take my word for it. If you wonder if James was the leader of the Jewish Christians or if the Gospel of Thomas was known as the fifth gospel, then simply look it up. There is plenty of support for the findings in this book.

Brahmacharya
(The Student)

During the first stage of life, a person prepares for career, family, and social responsibilities.

EARLY LIFE

My parents had four other children. Because I was the oldest child, I felt responsible for my siblings, and I have been a big brother longer than I have been anything else.

I lived in suburban Pittsburgh, where we explored the woods and played in the neighborhood. Pittsburgh had forests and hills and rivers, with cultural attractions, ethnic neighborhoods, and sports teams. It was a great place to grow up.

We moved often when I was in elementary school, so I was always the "new kid." Thus, I had low self-esteem, and I had a hard time making friends. Our parents pushed us, because they wanted us to go to good schools and get good jobs. My childhood was a blur, and I spent a lot more time fretting about my future than enjoying my youth.

SCOUTING

The Boy Scouts was one of the few places that gave me a real sense of belonging. Scouting teaches many valuable life lessons, and everyone pursues their own path.

I became an Eagle Scout. Along the way, I learned that the one in 100 boys who becomes an Eagle Scout is not the smartest or the strongest, but the most persistent, and this was a great life lesson. Scouting also provided different paths for different people.

Most important, Scouting allowed me to feel at home in the wilderness, and some of my best memories are the times that I have spent at beaches or deserts or forests. Appreciation for the outdoors has stayed with me.

EDUCATION

I was elected "Most Likely to Succeed" in high school and president of my fraternity in college. I was a good, but not great, student, because I was taught to conform, not to think. I gained knowledge, not wisdom, and I learned by repetition, not reflection.

College was a shock, and I was unprepared for life outside of my bubble. Entering college, I realized that not everyone is burdened by guilt or motivated by fear, and that there are other belief systems that are at least as valid as my own. In addition, having grown up with an absolute morality, I could see that most difficult moral decisions involve tradeoffs and that most choices are not simply right or wrong.

My college fraternity was one of the few places that gave me a sense of belonging. My fraternity contained an interesting mix of colorful characters with comical nicknames, and many of my fraternity brothers are still close friends, even 40 years after college.

I received the departmental award at the University of Virginia, where I studied city planning, and I received a full scholarship to graduate school at Syracuse University, where I studied public administration.

I was expected to go to college and to work in a professional field, which I did. Things have worked out well, but I often wonder if I was meant to be a park ranger, rather than an investment banker, and whether I would have been happier that way.

RELIGION

My parents raised us as Roman Catholics. In hindsight, we essentially had no spiritual life. We were "religious, but not spiritual." Richard Rohr, a Catholic priest, writes:

> I attended Catholic school where the reward/punishment, perfection/achievement system was used to maintain order. The God I was presented with was no unconditional lover, but that was the whole Catholic world in the 1950s. Reality

was shaped by a God who is punitive. It made for conformity and very little disruption.

The conditionality of this love was palpable. God loved us when we achieved, when we were perfect, but did he love us when we failed, when we missed the mark? Did our parents? Sadly, the Catholic world has not changed much since the 1950s for many of us.

Many Catholics believe that their religion is the correct and "original" religion, and the church implied that Jesus taught the first pope, who taught the next pope, and so on.

There were some absolute standards, some high expectations, and lots of guilt in Catholicism, and we were encouraged to embrace suffering (as Jesus suffered) and to look to the afterlife, where we would be punished or rewarded.

Before the Second Vatican Council in 1962, all Catholic Masses were said in Latin, and we were taught not to eat any meat on Fridays and to plan on spending some time in purgatory. After Vatican II, Masses were said in our native languages, dietary restrictions were loosened, and purgatory went out of fashion.

Although these were positive changes, since Catholic doctrine had been so absolute, some of us wondered what else might change and whether everything that we had been taught was really absolute, after all.

CHAPTER 1

WORLDVIEWS

WESTERN WORLDVIEW

Since religious ideas permeate all cultures, I was forced to broaden my perspective and to explore history, mythology, psychology, and science, among other topics. Soon, I found that the Western worldview is colored by Greek and Roman philosophy and Judeo-Christian theology, even if we are all not philosophers or theologians:

- The universe was created *ex nihilo,* out of nothing.

- There was a cosmic rift between God and humans, caused by original sin.

- God is personal, and he is omnipotent, omnipresent, and omniscient.

- Time is linear, not cyclical, and there is a beginning and an ending.

- The universe is orderly and purposeful; life has intrinsic meaning.

- Morality is absolute, and actions are either right or wrong.

- We have individual souls, and we may live beyond our physical lives.

- We have free will, and we may influence our lives and our afterlives.

A personal god is a being who can enjoy a relationship, like a person. Although many people in many places and many times believe in a higher power, the belief that God is a person (or three persons) is much more common in the Western worldview. From that standpoint, it is not accurate to say that we all believe in the same god.

Although the Hebrew Bible was fundamentally about the nation of Israel and the Christian Bible was fundamentally about the Kingdom of God, contemporary Christian beliefs emphasize personal responsibility and personal salvation, rather than communal responsibility and communal salvation, particularly in the United States.

The adage "God helps those who help themselves" is from *Poor Richard's Almanack,* not the Bible. Some say that God is actually more likely to help those who cannot help themselves.

Conventional ideas are deeply held and widely accepted, and we rarely question them, but if we are to discover universal Truth, rather than the truth in a particular tradition, then we need to examine some of these heretofore-unchallenged assumptions.

Many who believe in a personal god assume that there is an inherent meaning to life, but in *Conversations on Nonduality,* counselor Halina Pytlasinska writes, "We're trying to find meaning and purpose. It's like saying to a daffodil or a flower, 'Why are you here?' It's being life. Life doesn't need a purpose, or a goal or an objective, or an aim: life is life."

EASTERN WORLDVIEW

Eastern theology is colored by Chinese and Indian philosophy. Although it is difficult to generalize, partly because Eastern religions are not creedal and partly because Eastern religions do not agree among themselves, there are some assumptions that are more common to Eastern religions than to Western religions:

- The Universe is eternal, and it collapses and expands into and out of time.

- God is in everyone and everything, so a cosmic rift is not possible.

- God is impersonal, a force or presence that can be imagined as a person.

- Time is cyclical, not linear, and there is no beginning or ending.

- The Universe is orderly, possibly purposeful; we find our own meaning.

- Morality is relative, and right and wrong are functions of perspective.

- We exist in Oneness, and we return to the source when we die.

- We do not have free will, as we are impacted by chance, nature, and nurture.

Although free will is essential to the Western worldview, it is not essential to the Eastern worldview, and free will is problematic for scientists who study the brain. In fact, our thoughts come to us.

We do not decide to think, any more than we decide to breathe our air or digest our food. Most thoughts arise in our subconscious mind, and most conscious thoughts derive from nature or nurture. We are products of our conditioning, and we are slaves to our habits and instincts.

There are Christians who integrate Eastern worldviews in the Christian tradition, such as Bede Griffiths, a Benedictine monk who lived as a Hindu holy man at an ashram, and Ruben Habito, a former Jesuit priest who practices Catholicism and Zen Buddhism.

Meister Eckhart was a Christian mystic who is often compared to a Hindu sage or a Zen teacher in the way that he perceived the Christian God as if from an Eastern perspective:

> There is in the soul something which is above the soul,
> Divine, simple, a pure nothing; rather nameless than
> named, unknown than known.... It is absolute and free
> from all names and all forms, just as God is free and abso-
> lute in Himself.

Shankara was a prominent Hindu philosopher, who developed the nondual *Advaita Vedanta* philosophy, which has become a cornerstone of Eastern philosophy:

> I am other than name, form, and action. My nature is
> ever free! I am Self, the supreme unconditioned Brahman.
> I am pure Awareness, always nondual.

It is striking that two mystics from two dissimilar traditions could make two such similar statements.

CHAPTER 2

God

Most Christians believe that God is omnipotent, omnipresent, omniscient, but theologians have more nuanced views about God. Maybe God knows our past (but not our future) or our actions (but not our thoughts). Maybe God changes; maybe God suffers; maybe God co-creates the world with us, as Alfred North Whitehead and the process theologians say.

Religion is cultural. Typically, barren desert cultures are monotheistic, whereas fertile forest cultures are polytheistic. Typically, hunter-gatherer cultures are patriarchal and shamanic, and agricultural cultures are matriarchal and communal. Typically, patriarchal cultures worship male gods, and matriarchal cultures worship female gods. Some anthropologists believe that humans create God in their own image, not vice versa.

Different beliefs make sense to different people, according to their conditioning.

Different people (and different traditions) encounter the divine in different ways, and some non-Christian traditions practice profound and transformational ways of doing so.

Almost everyone who pursues a broad and deep exploration of other traditions will be moved by the compassion of Christianity, the devotion of Islam, the intellectual rigor of Judaism, the earthy practicality of Buddhism, or the rich vocabulary of Hinduism.

SECOND NAÏVETÉ

Philosopher Paul Ricœur described a maturity of human development known as a "second naïveté," where a person becomes more willing to embrace paradox. Catholic priest Richard Rohr explains, "This blessed simplicity is calm, knowing, patient, inclusive, and self-forgetful. It helps us move beyond anger, alienation, and ignorance. I believe this is the very goal of mature adulthood and mature religion."

When we encounter a reality that conflicts with our theology, do we conform our "reality" to match our theology or do we conform our theology to match our reality?

Some people are distressed by the idea that there may not be an intentional God who establishes rules and punishes or rewards us according to our respect for the rules. "But," they say, "that would mean that there is no justice, that we have no purpose."

Would there be justice without God? Sure, there are secular codes of conduct, as well as secular mechanisms to enforce them. Some combination of altruism, consequences, and self-interest can also foster justice without a law-giving God.

Maybe it is our role—in concert with God, or instead of God—to establish justice, and maybe it is our responsibility to find the meaning in our own lives. If that is reality, then we would do well to accept it, even if it conflicts with our theology.

BELIEFS

On the surface, there are major differences between the beliefs and practices of religions, but below the surface, the major religions are more similar than dissimilar when it comes to loving God and loving our fellow humans. In fact, because so much of religious belief and practice derives from culture, the biggest differences between religions arise from differences in cultures and worldviews.

Because beliefs are so important to Christianity, as compared to the other traditions, any spiritual journey should consider what we believe and why we believe it. Since some Christians believe that their beliefs and practices were revealed by God, any spiritual journey in the Western tradition should consider whether our beliefs more likely come from divine revelation or human speculation.

Despite the differences in beliefs and practices among the major traditions, there are many parallel sayings of Jesus and Muhammed and other spiritual leaders, so that if we are following Jesus, we are often following Buddha, Lao Tzu, and Muhammed, too.

As Henri Nouwen, a Catholic priest, wrote:

> Slowly, I came to realize that the differences between Catholic and Protestant, Christian and Buddhist, religious and secular, were not the kind of differences I thought they were; that there was a deeper unity below the surface.... To move from exclusive notions of Christian community to a more universal and inclusive vision of the human family of God is a difficult journey and requires a mature and confident faith.

It is interesting that Nouwen talked about a "confident faith." Halfway through my journey, my faith was not a confident faith, because I deconstructed my old beliefs without reconstructing my new beliefs. I was rejecting something, without embracing something else. Later in the book, I describe this dark night of the soul.

BELIEFS VERSUS PRACTICES

At the Society of Biblical Literature and American Academy of Religion, there are discussions among scholars about whether Jesus actually taught any of the parables, and at the Jesus Seminar, Bible scholars opine on which sayings Jesus actually said.

Believers would be surprised to learn that scholars doubt many passages in the Bible, thinking that they might have been added by authors, transcribers, or translators much later.

There is a surprising breadth and depth of theological inquiry that is informed by history and science. In 1966, there was a *Time* magazine cover on the "death of God," which was inspired by conversations that scholars were having about this theology. However, in church pews, pastors almost never ask these difficult questions.

An Episcopal priest was asked, "Do you still believe in God?" after he was ordained. Years later, he understood the profundity and relevance of the question—he saw that the more he learned about God, the more he knew he did not know.

Many people in the West think that religion is about beliefs, but most religions focus more on practices (orthopraxy) than beliefs (orthodoxy), and most religions are not as exclusive as Christianity. Most religions do not proscribe rigid beliefs and do not say that those with differing beliefs (inside or outside of their traditions) cannot be saved.

For example, Buddhism does not focus on philosophical questions, such as whether God exists, because these questions are speculative. Hinduism allows any number of contradictory beliefs, including atheism, monotheism, and polytheism.

The Eastern Orthodox church is much more mystical than its Western brethren. The Orthodox believe in deification or *theosis,* with the goal of seeking union with God. Clement of Alexandria, a leader in the early church, wrote, "The Son of God became man, so that we might become God," which sounds heretical to many Western Christians.

SOURCES OF BELIEFS

Christianity is seemingly all about beliefs or "faith," but many Christian beliefs do not come from God or Jesus or the Bible, but from Aristotle or Augustine or Aquinas. Aristotle was a Greek philosopher who lived in the fourth century BC, Augustine was a Catholic bishop who lived in the fourth century, and Aquinas was a Catholic theologian who lived in the thirteenth century.

Also, the Christian creeds did not develop until the late fourth century, and the comprehensive Catholic catechism or statement of beliefs did not appear until the 1500s, when Martin Luther aggressively challenged the Catholic beliefs of the time. (Luther began the Reformation and the ensuing split between Catholics and Protestants.)

For example, the idea of "traditional marriage" developed at the Council of Trent in 1545. The Council of Trent was an ecumenical council, a meeting of the Catholic bishops. After Luther questioned whether marriage was a sacrament, the Catholic church doubled down and insisted that it was a sacrament and that it was only valid if it was performed by a priest in a church.

"Fundamentalism" is largely a recent American experience. Church doctrine was increasingly scrutinized in the early 1900s, after discoveries in history and science, so conservative Christians published a series of pamphlets called "The Fundamentals." These pamphlets were published between 1900and 1915, many years after Jesus' death.

VARIETY OF BELIEFS

When I googled "what we believe," the search returned over six million hits, and most of them were statements by Christian churches or denominations who cannot agree on their beliefs.

In fact, there are almost 50,000 Christian denominations, so it is absurd to claim that any denomination, no matter how large or how old, contains the definitive Christian message, let alone anything like universal Truth.

Our beliefs are fluid too. A poll by the Public Religions Research Institute (PRRI) found that nearly one in four Americans previously followed a different denomination than they follow now.

Most Americans have no spiritual practice at all--60% percent never or seldom attend a religious service, 55% do not pray daily (including 34% who never or seldom pray) and 68% never or seldom read the Bible.

Many of those who DO believe in God DO NOT believe in the God of the Bible, and many of those who DO NOT believe in God DO believe in a higher power.

These lines are blurring. Christian authors, such as Brian McLaren, are writing books like *Do I Stay Christian?*, while atheist authors, such as Sam Harris, are writing books like *Waking Up: A Guide to Spirituality Without Religion*.

DEFENDING BELIEFS

The churches and colleges that protect these traditions are not very self-reflective. Catholic priests report to the Vatican, and Protestant ministers report to their churches or their denominations.

How does a pastor at a Christian church or a professor at a Christian college keep his or her job, while challenging conventional beliefs or expressing doubts about conventional beliefs?

Ask a Christian minister what he or she believes, and they may say something like, "As long as my church is paying my salary, then I believe what my church believes," hardly a hearty endorsement of Christian theology or an honest expression of personal beliefs.

Some Christians think that we should accept conventional beliefs at face value, even if they are superficial, supernatural, or superstitious. This type of blind faith creates an artificial tension between religion and science that does not need to exist. Rather than resist science (or resist religion), we can reconcile the two.

Most people do not come to church to ask difficult questions that challenge them. Instead, most people come to church to find simple answers that comfort them.

CHAPTER 3

THE GENTILES, PAGANS, AND ROMANS

The early writings about Jesus describe him as a wise man—a healer, a mystic, and a teacher. The later writings add mythological elements such as virgin birth, divine sonship, and physical resurrection, which were common features of the pagan religions.

THE GENTILES AND THE PAGANS

Most of the Roman world was pagan, meaning that they were not Christians or Jews. As Christianity spread through the pagan population and became the religion of the Roman Empire, it acquired pagan features.

Many pagan holy places were repurposed as Christian churches, many pagan holy days were repurposed as Christian holy days, and many pagan practices were repurposed as Christian practices—including altars, banquets, bells, blessings, candles, chants, fasting, holidays, icons, incense, pilgrimages, prayers, and vestments, as well as many funeral and wedding practices.

Much of Christian theology also derived from pagan sources. Greek philosophers, like Aristotle and Plato, influenced the concept of the *logos* or word, the doctrine of the Trinity, the focus on the afterlife, and the notion of the soul. The view that God is omnipotent, omnipresent, and omniscient is largely derived from Greek philosophy, too.

Anyone who studies mythology will recognize that many aspects of the Christian story are common archetypes in human history. Most primitive cultures developed creation stories and explanations for the presence of good and evil.

Also, many primitive cultures developed flood stories, such as the Mesopotamian story in the *Epic of Gilgamesh*, older than the Jewish story of Noah's flood in Genesis.

This writing was rediscovered less than 200 years ago, and until then, scholars were unaware of the similarities between the Book of Genesis and the *Epic of Gilgamesh*. There is also a creation narrative in the *Epic* that is similar to the Adam and Eve narrative.

Aspects of Jesus' life (virgin birth, divine sonship, sacrificial death, physical resurrection) are similar to those of other avatars and deities, such as Buddha, Krishna, and Osiris.

APOLLONIUS OF TYANA

In Jesus' time, there were messianic leaders, like Judah the Galilean and Simon bar Kokhba, and miracle workers, like Apollonius of Tyana and Honi the Circle-drawer.

Apollonius of Tyana was called the pagan Christ, and he lived in Jesus' time. Apollonius' followers believed that he was the son of a God and that he cast out spirits, healed the sick, performed miracles, and raised the dead. He was thought to be a savior, who descended to the underworld and ascended into heaven.

Some of Apollonius' writings still exist. Both he and Jesus are documented historical figures, but despite their similar trajectories, Jesus developed a following, and Apollonius did not. In ancient times, Eusebius, an early Christian historian, wrote a polemical tract against *The Life of Apollonius. The Life* and the tract were both written a century after Apollonius' death, when he was still being remembered in Christian circles.

THE ROMANS

In many Mediterranean cultures, such as the Egyptian, Greek, and Roman, there was a meeting of politics and religion, as rulers were considered divine or divinely appointed. In Egypt and Rome and other ancient cultures, the religion served to enhance the authority of the ruler and to strengthen his or her command.

Kingship was inherited, which is why the Jews looked to King David's descendants, and why both Jesus' and Mohammed's followers selected their relatives to succeed them. (Later in the book, we will discuss James, the brother of Jesus, who succeeded Jesus as the leader of the community that Jesus founded.)

In the first centuries, the Roman empire developed a state religion, an imperial cult that was focused on the emperors. The emperors were deified, and statues and temples were built in their honor. The emperors were called "lords," "saviors," and "sons of God."

As the Romans embraced Christianity, their new religion mirrored their old cult. The leader of the movement became the leader of the cult, and the church doctrine paralleled that of the ancient imperial cults. This was ironic, since Jesus initially resisted Roman rule, but the Romans eventually embraced Christianity.

ECUMENICAL COUNCILS

Emperor Constantine chaired the Council of Nicaea in AD 325. Constantine sought to unite the Roman empire under the banner of the church, by adopting a creed. For the first time, lines were drawn between orthodoxy and heresy, and those who disagreed lost their holdings, their positions, their state support, or their lives.

Over the next few centuries, several other ecumenical councils were convened, but they were not all well-attended, they were not all recognized by all church members, and they sometimes refuted conclusions that were reached at previous councils.

DOCTRINE OF ORIGINAL SIN

Much of Christian orthodoxy reflects theological speculation, such as the doctrine of original sin (which says that Adam's disobedience was passed on to his descendants). Although the Hebrew Bible describes the fall, the Jews do not believe in original sin. This doctrine was not known until Augustine developed it, 400 years after Jesus' death.

The doctrine of original sin has a chilling effect on Christian theology by creating a cosmic rift between God and humans. Some Protestant churches believe that original sin suggests that man is subject to "total depravity." No wonder Martin Luther and others believed that man should not seek union with God through mysticism.

Some Christians believe that original sin had something to do with sexuality, but the sin in Genesis was actually eating the fruit of the tree of knowledge of good and evil. Augustine was preoccupied with sex, and his misogynistic views colored his theology.

When we embrace the knowledge of good and evil, we introduce dualism, distinction, and separation. We distinguish between ourselves and God and between ourselves and others. These distinctions do not exist in more nondual worldviews. When we make these and other distinctions (a role that had belonged to God alone in the story of Adam and Eve), we judge ourselves and others.

Rupert Spira, a spiritual teacher, writes, "In the Christian tradition, the mistake is referred to as the 'original sin.' It is the original mistake, the result of which the story of a separate entity that exists in time is born." For Spira and others, there is no separation.

DOCTRINE OF THE TRINITY

Likewise, the doctrine of the Trinity was not known until Tertullian developed it, 300 years after Jesus' death. Tertullian was an apologist who defended orthodox views, and a polemicist who attacked those whom he considered to be heretics.

The first mention of the Trinity was in the second century, when Theophilus of Antioch defined it as God, His Word (*Logos*), and His

Wisdom. It is really interesting that Theophilus did not include Jesus or the Holy Spirit in the original Trinity.

Logos is a Greek philosophical term for the creative power of the Universe, and Wisdom is the feminine personification of divine wisdom. *Logos* and Wisdom are mentioned in the Christian Bible and the Hebrew Bible as God's companions, not as gods. The Gospel of John appears to elevate *Logos* to divine status and to identify Jesus with *Logos*, but these are John's words, and they were written many years after Jesus' death.

Feminists note that *Sophia* (the Greek word for "wisdom") is feminine. Although Jesus was said to personify Wisdom, some Christian churches resist the idea of female priests or ministers because Jesus was a male. However, in the early Christian churches, females assumed leadership roles, led missions, provided funds, and served as deacons.

There is no mention of a Trinity in either the Christian Bible or the Hebrew Bible. Although Jesus mentioned the Father and the Holy Spirit, he did not say that Jesus or the Holy Spirit were divine, and he taught his disciples to pray to the Father only.

Jesus was not decreed as God by the church until the Council of Nicaea in AD 325, and the Holy Spirit was not decreed as God by the church until the Council of Constantinople in AD 381. Some Christians assume that these were mere formalities, but the Trinity was fiercely debated for centuries, both before and after these councils.

In the fourth century, the Catholic bishops undertook some theological gymnastics to reconcile the divinity and humanity of Jesus, drawing distinctions between "natures" and "persons" who are somehow both different and the same. By torturous reasoning, they decreed that it was orthodoxy to say that "Jesus is one nature, divine and human," but that it was heresy to say that "Jesus is two natures, one divine and one human."

The doctrine of the Trinity can be a helpful way of describing the indescribable, in thinking of God as transcendent (the Father) and immanent (the Holy Spirit), as personified by an avatar (Jesus).

The Hindu Trinity of God as creator, sustainer, and destroyer serves a similar purpose. However, if we take either doctrine literally, in saying that God is personal or that God is limited by these three particular persons, then we have abandoned a helpful description in favor of a tenuous speculation.

DOCTRINE OF
SUBSTITUTIONARY ATONEMENT

Likewise, the doctrine of substitutionary atonement, which suggests that Jesus' death was meant to satisfy God for the sin of man, was developed by Anselm and Aquinas, 1,000 years and 1,200 years after Jesus' death, respectively. During the medieval period, people thought that if a serf offended the king, then the king would exact compensatory payment. In today's democratic societies, we no longer believe barbaric, medieval ideas like this.

Progressive Christians believe that Jesus taught us how to live, not how to die, and that Jesus' death was tragic and unnecessary. Would Jesus' life have been meaningful, if he had not died at the hands of the Romans? Absolutely.

JESUS' DOCTRINE

We have to wonder why Jesus did not mention any of this doctrine in his ministry. If it was important for us to know that he was born of a virgin, or that he was divine, or that we were all stained by original sin, or that he would die in substitutionary atonement, or that he would be physically resurrected, or that we are saved by faith or grace or works, why did he not say so?

I know Christians who believe that the Bible is inerrant, the inspired word of God, until Jesus says something that contradicts their own theology or that of their church. Then, they might say: Perhaps Jesus forgot. Perhaps Jesus was misunderstood. Perhaps Jesus was misquoted. Perhaps Jesus was speaking specifically to one person, not generally to the rest of us.

Imagine that Augustine, Tertullian, Anselm, and Aquinas were wrong and that their theories of original sin, the Trinity, and substitutionary atonement are false. With no cosmic rift, there was no need for atonement, and no reason for Jesus to die. Much of Christian theology would erode, since it is based on these theories, not on Jesus' words.

CHAPTER 4

THE JEWS AND THE JEWISH CHRISTIANS

J esus was a Jew. Peter and Paul and James were Jews. The apostles were Jews, and all of Jesus' early followers were Jews.

Scholars agree that Jesus intended to reform Judaism; Jesus never intended to start Christianity or any other religion. In fact, he was skeptical of organized religion, arguing with Pharisees, Sadducees, priests, and scribes alike.

Many Bible scholars agree that Christianity was founded by Paul, rather than Jesus, and that Jesus (who never wrote anything) and Paul, Matthew, Mark, Luke, and John (who wrote much of the New Testament) each had their own conflicting theologies.

MONOTHEISM

Around 600 BC, the Babylonians conquered the Jews and exiled them to Babylon. Babylon was the largest city in the world and the center of the Babylonian empire. There, the Jews acquired dualistic notions about good and evil, heaven and hell, and angels and devils from the Zoroastrians, and the Christians later adopted these ideas.

Zoroastrians were followers of Zoroaster or Zarathustra, known as the first monotheist. Zoroastrian ideas about the Saoshyant—the final savior, who would conquer the forces of evil and resurrect the bodies of the dead, making the world immortal and perfect—influenced Jewish ideas about the Messiah.

If you ask a modern Zoroastrian if he believes in heaven and hell, he might say that ancient believers view them literally, but modern believers view them metaphorically. This is interesting, since many contemporary Christians view them literally, but many Zoroastrians, who originated them, and some Jews, who adopted them, do not.

Until the Babylonian exile, the Jews were polytheists who worshipped many gods. One was Asherah, a mother goddess who was likely worshipped as the consort of Yahweh. Initially, Yahweh was a tribal god, and the Jews knew that other tribes had gods, too.

Eventually, the Jews came to believe that their god was the only God, but this may not have happened until 200 BC. Jesus and his followers would likely not have believed that God is three persons, since the theory of the Trinity had not been developed yet.

THE HEBREW BIBLE AND
THE CHRISTIAN BIBLE

The Hebrew Bible is incorporated into the Christian Bible, and some Christians believe that the New Testament "completes" the Old Testament. Jews do not believe this, just as Christians do not believe that the Book of Mormon completes the Christian Bible.

Likewise, some Christians believe that the Hebrew Bible foreshadows Jesus, but Jews do not believe this either. Passages in the Hebrew Bible that might refer to Jesus have other meanings for Jewish readers, who do not see hints of Jesus in their scriptures.

In Jesus' time, Judaism was a pluralistic religion. Pharisees, Sadducees, and Jewish Christians worshipped in the temple, even though these sects had different beliefs. For example, the Pharisees believed in life after death, whereas the Sadducees did not.

Writer Rachel Held Evans contrasted Christian and Jewish approaches to scripture, writing, "While Christians tend to turn to scripture to end a conversation, Jews turn to scripture to start a conversation."

Generally, Jews are more metaphorical and more pluralistic in their theology than Christians. It seems that is more common for a Jew than it is for a Christian to question the historical accuracy of an account or the literal interpretation of a passage, and Jewish scholars are more likely to recognize alternative meanings of certain passages.

Many Jewish scholars question the historical existence of people like Adam, Abraham, Moses, and Noah, as well as the historicity of events such as the exodus and the flood.

Many Christian scholars question these things, too, and some Christian laypeople may be alarmed to learn that many biblical characters might not have lived, and that many biblical events might not have happened.

For years, many Christians and Jews believed that Moses wrote the Pentateuch (the first five books of the Hebrew Bible), but most scholars reject that theory today, particularly since these books actually describe Moses' death.

THE JEWISH CHRISTIANS

After Jesus' death, most Catholics believe that Peter, the "first pope," was the leader of the Christian community. The notion that Jesus founded the church "upon this rock" is essential to the Catholic understanding of the church, but there is no evidence that Peter ever served as Bishop of Rome or that he ever lived in Rome. (He might have died there though.)

Some Protestants believe that Paul, the author and evangelist, was the leader of the Christian community, because of his prominence in the New Testament, but they realize that he disagreed with other church leaders and that he was itinerant.

There is no evidence that Paul ever led the Christian community. Rather, Paul reported to the others, and the Acts of the Apostles describes the Council of Jerusalem, where Gentiles (or those who were not Jewish) were permitted to join the movement.

JAMES THE JUST

The actual leader of the Jewish Christian community was James the Just, the brother of Jesus, who served for more than 30 years. James was called the "bishop of bishops, who rules Jerusalem, the Holy Assembly of Hebrews, and all assemblies everywhere," in a fourth century letter ascribed to the first century church father, Clement of Rome.

The Gospel of Thomas was recovered in 1945, but it was written around the same time as the canonical gospels. In this gospel, which some scholars call "the fifth gospel," the disciples asked Jesus before his ascension, "We are aware that you will depart from us. Who will be our leader?" Jesus said to them, "No matter where you come [from] it is to James the Just that you shall go, for whose sake heaven and earth have come to exist."

In the Acts of the Apostles, James was respected and trusted by all, including Peter and Paul. James presided over the Council of Jerusalem, which agreed to accept Gentiles as community members. He received the report that Peter escaped from prison. He met Paul on his trip to Jerusalem, and he accepted Paul's offering from the gentile churches.

The Jewish Christians continued to worship in the temple, and James was said to have thick calluses on his knees from praying. They likely believed that Jesus was the Messiah, but not divine, and they baptized in his name and shared a meal in his memory.

The belief in Jesus' divinity increased as the church became less Jewish and more gentile. There was no Jewish understanding that the Messiah would be divine, and Jews, unlike Greeks and Romans, did not accept that people could have divine *and* human origins.

Then, everything changed. James was killed in AD 62. We do not know when either Peter or Paul was killed, but scholars estimate that they both died before AD 64. Jerusalem was destroyed in AD 70. Christians and Jews went their own ways, and the earliest Christians—along with James, their leader—were forgotten in the next 300 years.

THE SPLIT BETWEEN THE
CHRISTIANS AND THE JEWS

The Jews met in Yavneh, a city in central Israel, where they reimagined Judaism, after the Temple—which had served as the focus of their religion—was destroyed. At Yavneh, Judaism was reimagined as Rabbinic Judaism, which is based on the oral Torah and the written Torah, both said to be revealed by God to Moses.

The Christian bishops met in ecumenical councils, where they created Christian doctrine that forms the basis of the creeds that are recited in Christian churches today.

Just as the Christians and the Jews retreated to their corners and drew lines, many years later the Roman Catholics and the Eastern Orthodox would separate, and the Catholics and the Protestants would separate. In fact, the tendency to splinter arises in many traditions, including Buddhism, Hinduism, and Islam.

Consider that Jesus' ministry lasted for three years, James' leadership lasted for 30 years, and the Jewish Christians and the Gentile Christians lived for the next 300 years without a Bible or a creed or an orthodoxy.

Most church histories jump from Jesus' death in AD 33 to the Council of Nicaea in AD 325, with nary a mention of the earliest years, and it is unfortunate that we know so little about the earliest Christians and their beliefs and practices.

Grihastha
(The Householder)

During the second stage of life, a person marries, pursues a career, and raises a family. Spiritual practice is important, but material comfort is important, too.

FAMILY

I married Jill, my high school sweetheart, and we moved to Arizona and Texas, where we raised two children, Lauren and Marc, who both married and raised children themselves.

I cared about my family and friends, but I gave almost no thought to anyone else, mostly because I was busy pursuing a career and raising a family. I was not at all insightful or reflective, and I accepted everything that my parents and priests said.

My life was superficial, not spiritual. My spiritual life, such as it was, consisted of spending one hour every week falling asleep to a boring homily and reciting responses to a lifeless liturgy among a few dozen uninspired people who barely knew each other.

LOCAL GOVERNMENT

For the first five years of my career, I worked in local government, mostly at a council of governments, where representatives from local governments discussed regional problems.

Although I had a good perspective on the problems of the region and the problems of each of the cities, if you asked me what I did for a living, I would have had to admit, "Actually, I go to meetings for a living."

I realized that I had to develop mastery. I had to find something to sell that someone wanted to buy. Also, I realized that I was technically oriented, so I liked to figure out things, and that I was institutionally oriented, so that I liked to figure out big things.

I set my sights on becoming a public finance investment banker, helping state and local governments to borrow money for capital projects and cash flow needs, and I went to the local university library, where I read every book on the public finance shelf.

INVESTMENT BANKING

Investment banking, like spiritual practice, is both experiential and intellectual, and investment banking is a transactional business.

I lived a transactional life, making deals with God and my parents, and (later) with my schools and my workplaces. Somehow, I always knew what I needed to give up to get what I wanted. In our achievement-oriented, individualistic, and materialistic society, my life was not that unusual, but it was certainly not generous or selfless or wholesome.

In investment banking, I saw people as "clients" or "potential clients." Today, when I explain my transformation to people, I say that in the past, I rarely socialized with people unless we were discussing a transaction. Work/life balance is a common problem, but my life was more lopsided than most.

APPRENTICESHIP, JOURNEYMAN, MASTER

The investment banking business is pretty competitive and pretty mercenary. As soon as I started, I discovered that "all of the dogs have peed on all of the trees" and that the only work left for a newcomer was the most complicated, difficult financings.

I said to myself, "For the next five years, call me anything you want and pay me anything you want, and let me handle the stuff that nobody else wants to do. In five years, I'll be the most valuable guy in the building, and I'll write my own ticket."

For five years, I focused my energies on learning all that I could about finance. Later, author Malcom Gladwell determined that 10,000 hours of practice makes an expert. (Interestingly, 10,000 hours approximately equals five years of 40-hour workweeks.)

A professional career is like a spiritual practice, and one does not attain mastery without effort. Also, one is never done growing or learning.

Investment bankers are only paid if they can close deals, so I learned how to close, distinguishing quickly between potential deals that could close and those that could not and finding creative ways to go around, over, or through any obstacle.

Soon, I developed a sixth sense for seeing the financing that might emerge from a situation, like a sculptor seeing the statue that might emerge from a block of marble. Shortly, I was promoted from "associate" to "principal" to "managing director," which roughly means from "apprentice" to "journeyman" to "master," and I was making five times as much money as I was making going to meetings in government.

ORGANIZED RELIGION

My spiritual journey began in my 40s. I thought I would become a deacon in the church, and I taught classes for young people who wanted to be married by a priest. Also, I served on the Diocesan Pastoral Council, where I witnessed the struggle between our old bishop, who embraced reform, and our new bishop, who did not.

I wrestled with some Catholic teachings, and I was shocked and outraged by the clergy abuse crisis and the church's reactionary and unconscionable responses to it. Also, I was perplexed that the Catholic clergy, who had committed so many unspeakable acts, could be so casual about their own misbehavior and so urgent about others' misbehavior.

Although my wife was not raised Catholic, she attended Mass with me for 40 years, until a new priest said, "If you are not Catholic, you are NOT welcome at communion." Jesus welcomed sinners, but Catholics do not even welcome non-Catholics at communion. That was the last time that we set foot in a Catholic church.

This is one of the most damaging of Catholic teachings, and it later shamed me that I had accepted the Church's intolerance of my divorced, LGBTQ, and non-Catholic friends. Was I bothered by intolerance only when it was my own family that was being hurt?

In time, we attended a Disciples of Christ church. The denomination was tolerant, but the congregation was not, and an elder confronted me because my evolving beliefs were not conventional enough for his taste. Pharisees, Sadducees, and Jewish Christians all worshipped at the temple in Jesus' day, but those with different views are not welcome now. That was the last time that we set foot in a Protestant church.

I had 50 years of experience with organized religion, and the particular situations that triggered both of my exits were (sadly) ordinary. In fact, the exclusivity and the intolerance are features, not bugs, of contemporary Christianity. Eventually, I decided that enough was enough, and I left.

I was angry that my church experience had been so inhospitable. As Gandhi said, "I like your Christ. I do not like your Christians. Your Christians are so unlike your Christ." Could we follow Jesus without belonging to a church? Absolutely.

CHAPTER 5

The Gospels

Many modern scholars recognize that the Bible is a great telling of stories, not an accurate retelling of history, and this is not meant as a criticism. The Bible is powerful, whether it is interpreted literally or allegorically, metaphorically, or mythically.

As Christianity absorbed gentile and pagan influences, the new religion departed from its Jewish roots in adopting Jesus' divinity and in embracing pagan mythologies. Further, the gospels were not written by eyewitnesses, and each has its own theology.

The Gospel of Mark is inclusive ("If they are not against us, they are with us"), while the Gospel of Matthew is exclusive ("If they are not with us, they are against us").

The empty tomb of Mark devolves into the mystical theology of John in 80 years, and Jesus' focus on the Father devolves into the gospel writers' focus on Jesus himself. Also, the divinity of Jesus, which would have been anathema to the Jewish Christians, came to be accepted as Christianity succumbed to pagan influences.

My deconstruction involved taking a good, hard look at the gospels, side-by-side. Obviously, John's mystical theology is a long way from Mark's empty tomb.

GOSPEL OF MARK
(THE FIRST GOSPEL)

The Gospel of Mark was written around AD 70, 40 years after Jesus' death and several years after James' death. Mark is relatively straightforward and unadorned.

There is no virgin birth account, no genealogy, and no post-resurrection appearances in the Gospel of Mark. (Many Bibles note or omit the so-called longer ending, which contains post-resurrection appearances, because it did not appear in the earliest copies and is considered to be a later addition.) Jesus denies that he is the Son of God, and scholars call his denial the "messianic secret." In this gospel, Jesus is a human figure:

- There is no virgin birth account.
- There is no genealogy.
- John baptizes Jesus for the forgiveness of sins.
- Jesus is called Christ or Son of God, but commands his followers not to disclose it.
- Jesus does not appear after his death.

The Gospels of Matthew and Luke differ from Mark, although they are both based on Mark, and on other material that historians call the *quelle* ("source") or "Q" document. If this common source material once existed in manuscript form, it has since been lost. Because of their similarities, these first three gospels are known as the synoptic gospels.

GOSPEL OF MATTHEW
(THE JEWISH GOSPEL)

The Gospel of Matthew was written between AD 80 and 110, up to 80 years after Jesus' death. Matthew incorporates Jewish themes and emphasizes the significance of Jesus in Jewish history. This gospel was written for Jewish readers.

The Gospel of Matthew was the Jewish Gospel. There are *new* virgin birth and genealogy accounts that compare Jesus to Moses and echo Old Testament themes. Also:

- There is an incident at Jesus' birth that parallels the slaughter of the innocents in the Hebrew Bible.

- There is a genealogy that traces Jesus' lineage back to Abraham.

- John baptizes Jesus, but suggests that he is not worthy to do so.

- Jesus is called the Son of Man. He is mocked as the Son of God, but he answers to it.

- Jesus appears after his death, at the tomb and in Galilee.

GOSPEL OF LUKE
(THE GENTILE/PAGAN GOSPEL)

The Gospel of Luke was written between AD 80 and 100, up to 70 years after Jesus' death. Luke addresses an audience broader than Matthew's audience. For example, he traces Jesus' ancestry to Adam, not only Abraham, and emphasizes the significance of Jesus in human history, not only Jewish history.

The Gospel of Luke was the gentile gospel. There are *different* virgin birth and genealogy accounts that compare Jesus to Adam and emphasize universal themes. Also:

- There is a virgin birth account, in which Jesus is adored by shepherds.

- There is a genealogy that traces Jesus back to Adam.

- Jesus is baptized, but it is not clear who did it or why they did it.

- Jesus is called Christ or Lord or Savior or Son of God.

- Jesus appears after his death, at the tomb, on the road, and in Jerusalem.

(Terms like "Lord," "Messiah," "Son of God," and "Son of Man" are certainly honorific terms, but 2,000 years ago, they did not mean that Jesus was divine. A lord was a master; a messiah was an earthly ruler; a son of God was a pious person; and a son of man was a human. Today, many associate these terms with the Trinity, which came 300 years later.)

GOSPEL OF JOHN
(THE MYSTICAL GOSPEL)

The Gospel of John was written between AD 90 and 110, up to 80 years after Jesus' death. Imagine writing a book about your great, great grandfather, 80 years after his death. Do you even know his name?

Some Christian apologists argue that oral culture was good at preserving traditions, but New Testament scholar Bart D. Ehrman argues that no one who studied oral culture ever said that. Word of mouth is typically unreliable.

John introduced the theory that Jesus existed prior to creation, so there are *no* birth or genealogy accounts. In contrast to Mark's messianic secret, Jesus calls himself the Bread of Life; the Light of the World; the Way, the Truth, and the Life.

John does not resemble the synoptic gospels in content, style, or theology. John primarily takes place in Jerusalem, not Galilee, and the Easter chronology is unique. Also, in John, Jesus speaks in long discourses, rather than short aphorisms and proverbs.

John describes a "high Christology" or an elevated view of Jesus, and if we read the documents in the order that they were written, we realize that Jesus became increasingly mythologized and romanticized. John was written for Christian believers. In this gospel, Jesus is a divine figure:

- There is no virgin birth account, because Jesus was said to exist prior to creation.

- There is no genealogy, because Jesus' divine nature was emphasized.

- There is no baptism account, because Jesus could not be baptized by any person.

- Jesus is called Messiah or Prophet or Savior and many metaphorical names.

- Jesus appears after his death, at the tomb and in the Upper Room (twice).

John deemphasizes Jesus' human nature and emphasizes his divine nature, although Jesus' divinity was barely mentioned (if at all) in the earlier gospels. Also, some scholars believe that the author of the Gospel of John was also the author of Revelation, the last book in the New Testament, which describes the second coming of Christ.

Most of the other gospels assumed that Jesus' return was imminent, that he would return within their lifetimes. It only became necessary to describe the future coming of Christ when he did not return promptly, as his early followers believed that he would.

(Terms like "Bread of Life," "the Light of the World," and "the Way, the Truth, and the Life" are honorific and metaphorical, but they did not mean that Jesus was divine.)

If Jesus and the Father are one, are they of one mind or of one nature? If Jesus spoke these words 80 years before, why is there no mention of them in any of the other gospels, which were written much earlier? Perhaps either much of John is elaboration or much of the other gospels is faulty recollection.

When I read the gospels side by side, I was surprised by their different voices, their factual differences, and their varying views of Jesus. Either the later gospels incorporated material that was not original (which seems to me the likeliest explanation), or the later gospels recovered original material that had been lost in the earlier years.

Why would earlier gospels omit key material, if they are inspired or revealed by God?

In 1993, the Jesus Seminar, a collection of progressive New Testament scholars, attained fame (or infamy) when they released *The Five Gospels,* a search for the authentic words of Jesus. The scholars questioned almost 80 percent of the words attributed to Jesus, and they questioned almost all of the words in the Gospel of John.

In 2016, I attended a seminar on the parables of Jesus, held at the annual meeting of the Society of Biblical Literature and American Academy of Religion. The seminar featured a distinguished panel of New Testament scholars. One panelist summarized their findings about the veracity of the parables by saying that some scholars accept all of the parables, some scholars reject all of the parables, and most scholars accept some of the parables as Jesus' actual words.

Given the conflicts between the Gentile Christians and the Jewish Christians, especially since the destruction of the Temple and the death of Jesus' brother James, we might expect that Christianity would stray from its monotheistic Jewish roots and embrace the gentile beliefs and practices of many of its new followers, and that happened.

GOSPEL OF THOMAS
(THE SO-CALLED FIFTH GOSPEL)

The Gospel of Thomas, like the Q document, does not contain birth accounts, genealogies, or post-resurrection appearances, nor does it contain any supernatural miracles. This Gospel is a "sayings" gospel, and it repeats many sayings from the first three gospels.

We do not know whether the Gospel of Thomas was written before or after the others, but it likely reflects early Christian views, so it is puzzling that it was not contained in the Bible. It is possible that this gospel was hidden by its proponents or ignored by its opponents, because its theology is so different from the other gospels.

CHAPTER 6

The Gentile Christians

LETTER OF JAMES

Although we do not know whether James was written by James or by a follower, it could be one of the earliest books, and it does not contain birth accounts, genealogies, or post-resurrection appearances, nor does it mention healings, miracles, or the resurrection.

For these reasons (and because James challenged Paul's theology), Martin Luther called the Letter of James "an epistle of straw," and he wanted to purge it from the Bible.

This is shocking, given that James led the Christian community for 30 years. Whether James was written by James or by a follower, it seems to reflect an early and important Christian perspective, which was likely representative of beliefs of the early Jewish Christians.

LETTERS OF PAUL

Likewise, the letters of Paul were probably among the earliest books written, they contain no birth accounts and no genealogies, and they recount no miracles. In fact, Paul says almost nothing about Jesus' life or teachings, focusing on his resurrection.

Some letters attributed to Paul may have been written by others, so it can be difficult to determine which words that are attributed to

Paul are actually his words. Because he wrote so much of the New Testament, Paul is seen as a seminal figure, but he never met Jesus during Jesus' life, and he sometimes disagreed with the other leaders.

THE DIDACHE

The Lord's Teaching through the Twelve Apostles to the Nations, commonly called the Didache, is a first century Jewish Christian statement of belief and practice. Whenever the Didache mentions Jesus in prayer, he is called "your servant Jesus." Otherwise, except for the baptismal ritual, Jesus is not even mentioned in the book, suggesting that Jesus was not the focus of worship among the Jewish Christians.

The book was itself an early document, and scholars suggest that it came from an even earlier one, reflecting the views of early Jewish Christians. It is known as the first statement of Christian beliefs, so it is an authoritative document.

HISTORY OR MYTHOLOGY

Throughout the gospels, Jesus performs miracles, which are now read allegorically, metaphorically, and mythically rather than literally, by many modern Bible scholars.

The later gospels contain more supernatural events than the earlier gospels. For example, Jesus raises the dead in all four gospels, but he raises Lazarus four days later, not immediately, in the Gospel of John. There were no miracles in the early sources, including the Didache, Q, the Gospel of Thomas, the Letter of James, and the Letters of Paul.

In the gospels, Jesus is referred to as Lord, Messiah, Son of God, and Son of Man. Certainly, these were very honorific terms, but they did not suggest that Jesus was divine. Today, many Christians hear these terms in a trinitarian context, but they were not written to suggest that Jesus was a member of the Trinity, a concept created much later.

The genealogies in Matthew and Luke are not complete or consistent or correct. Between David and Jesus, Matthew lists 28 generations, and Luke lists 42 generations. Likewise, Luke lists 76 generations between Adam and Jesus, which is only 2,000 years, but scientists agree that human beings have been on Earth for more than 200,000 years.

In some of Jesus' appearances after death, he does not appear in his earthly form. During his appearances, he is not recognized by his disciples, or he walks through walls, or he cannot be touched because he has not ascended, so these sightings might not be physical events.

The Bible says that Jesus was put to death in flesh, but resurrected in spirit. Paul recounts several post-resurrection appearances where Jesus appears to others, including Paul himself, but we know that Paul witnessed a *vision,* not a physical event.

Death and resurrection are common themes in primitive religions, especially in agricultural societies, and the three days that Jesus spent in the tomb and that Jonah spent in the belly of the whale parallel the three days that the moon disappears during the New Moon.

It seems likely that Jesus' three days in the tomb are mythical, not literal, and the fact that the gospels differ on when Jesus was buried and when the empty tomb was found further suggests that the gospels are telling a story, not retelling a history.

If we believe that God intervenes in human affairs, then we can believe all manner of supernatural events—such as virgin births and physical resurrections—that would otherwise seem unbelievable. However, if we admit that there is no solid evidence that God intervenes in human affairs, then these events can seem preposterous.

OTHER INFLUENCES

Most Christians believe that contemporary Christian beliefs are absolute, authentic, original, rational, unchanging, and universal, without realizing:

- Christianity borrowed from mythologies of Greeks, Romans, and other cultures.

- Christianity borrowed from Judaism and other religions.

- Christianity was unstructured for the first 300 years of its history.

- Different theologies are reflected in the Bible and the earliest writings.

- Many beliefs changed between the first gospel and the last gospel.

- Many beliefs were developed very recently.

In 2021, the Westar Institute released *After Jesus Before Christianity*, debunking the idea that the current framework of Christianity is 2,000 years old, writing, "Unlike historical assumptions of 40 years ago, it no longer makes sense to think of the second century as a time in which orthodoxy was establishing itself and what was later thought of as heresy was being dismantled."

If you place Christianity next to other ancient religions, you might say, "Aha, the myth of the creation… aha, the myth of the fall… aha, the myth of the flood… aha, the myth of the virgin birth… aha, the myth of the divine sonship… aha, the myth of the resurrection," etc. These myths seem unique only because most other ancient religions have not survived.

Imagine that the gospels were not written as objective reporting of history, but as subjective interpretations of some allegorical, metaphorical, and mythical memories. These memories of Jesus became more mythologized and romanticized as time went on.

Imagine that Christianity was lost to the ages, like so many other ancient religions, and that archaeologists recently discovered the Bible. If our beliefs were not embedded in our culture for the last 2,000 years, would we accept at face value that Jesus was divine, that he was born of a virgin, and that he was resurrected from the dead, or would we conclude that Jesus was one of many ancient holy men who became mythologized?

CHAPTER 7

THE CATHOLICS AND THE PROTESTANTS

THE CATHOLICS

In some ways, the Catholic church began at the Council of Nicaea in AD 325, where the emperor and the Catholic bishops defined Christian beliefs, drew distinct lines between orthodoxy and heresy, and placed these orthodox beliefs at the center of the new religion.

ORTHODOXY AND HERESY

The Nicene Creed, accepted by most Christians, is inspired by Greek philosophy. Jesus is "begotten not made, one in being with the Father...." Could Jesus be "made not begotten" or "begotten and made" or "neither begotten nor made?"

There was a lot of splitting of hairs concerning words like *ousia* or "essence," which identified the common nature of the Trinity, and *hypostasis* or "person," which identified the unique personalities of the individual persons of the Trinity.

Many modern scholars believe that the Trinity is an awkward compromise that appeased everyone without resolving anything, and the idea that a man can be a God made more sense in ancient times, when the Egyptians and the Greeks and the Romans mythologized demigods and heroes who were said to be born of couplings between gods and humans.

Ancient people argued about things that modern people would never argue about. It is orthodoxy to believe that Jesus is one substance (singly fully divine and fully human) but it is heresy to believe that Jesus is two substances (both fully divine and fully human). Clearly, this is an awkward and unworkable compromise that explains nothing.

BELIEF VERSUS TRUST

Does any of this matter? Does anyone live life differently if Jesus is one substance or two? At this point in the discussion, a fundamentalist Christian might say, "We must have faith," as if it is helpful to believe unbelievable things, without bothering to explain them.

In Christianity, the concept of "faith" has been corrupted. The Greek word for faith, *pistis*, means "trust; faithfulness; involvement," not acceptance of a creed.

Paul Tillich was a Christian philosopher who wrote about faith. According to Tillich, faith is not "an act of knowledge that has a low degree of evidence… Faith is more than trust in authorities, although trust is an important element of faith." Later, he dismissively wrote, "Here absurdity replaces thought, and faith is called the acceptance of absurdities." Tillich said that real faith is a matter of "ultimate concern," where faith relates to character, not content. Faith is a way of being, not a set of beliefs.

In *Theology Without Walls*, author Rory McEntee writes:

> To see faith as something that exists prior to every belief system is to turn on its head a more widespread, pedestrian understanding of faith, where "faith" exhibits a "belief" in something that perhaps cannot be proven, like the trinitarian nature of God, for instance. If, on the other hand, faith *precedes* any belief system, then it stems not from assent to some humanly constructed religious framework, but rather exists as an intrinsic aspect of humanity's entanglement with ultimacy.

APOSTOLIC SUCCESSION

When I was Catholic, we were supposed to believe in apostolic succession, the notion that the bishops were successors to the apostles in an unbroken chain. However, succession was not unbroken, and the history of the church was a broken chain of heretic popes, multiple popes, and popes and bishops who bought or inherited their offices.

It is possible to trace the succession of each bishop, but the chain only extends from the Reformation, when the legitimacy of the bishops was first questioned. Accordingly, the church requires that several bishops attend the ordination of new bishops, to reduce the likelihood of installing bishops who are not successors to the apostles.

Much of the church's doctrine was developed at the Council of Trent in 1545, which was the beginning of the Counter-Reformation, and much of this doctrine was developed in response to Protestantism. Until then, the Catholic church had no comprehensive catechism.

The catechism is a 600-page book that establishes all of the church's teachings. Once we realize that we do not know anything about God, then we see that a catechism is speculation and that it is as possible to introduce errors as it is to reveal truth.

The Catholic church (and the Protestant church) expresses its beliefs firmly. When the church is wrong, as it was in attacking Galileo, it can take centuries to correct. In recent years, the church has changed its mind about several beliefs, such as purgatory, which leads some Catholics to wonder, "What else is the church wrong about?"

PAPAL INFALLIBILITY

Papal infallibility, which is the doctrine that the Pope cannot err when he teaches on faith and morals, began at the First Vatican Council, 1,900 years after Jesus' death. Pope Pius IX stated that Mary, the mother of Jesus, was conceived without original sin.

This is curious, since the Pope's statement, which is considered to be infallible, is based on Augustine's concept of original sin, which is itself only a theory.

The doctrine of papal infallibility evolved over time. For years, the Bishop of Rome was "just another bishop," and he was not present at some of the ecumenical councils, nor did he preside over all of them. Papal primacy contributed to a major split in the church. The Catholic church believes that the pope has "full, supreme, and universal power over the church," whereas the Orthodox church believes that the pope is "first among equals," retaining the original view.

THE PROTESTANTS

Protestantism began at the Reformation, more than 1,500 years after Jesus' death. Although many Protestants believe that the Catholics altered the "original" religion, and that the Protestants restored it, the Protestants introduced many alterations, too.

BIBLICAL INERRANCY

I attended a Protestant church for several years. Many Protestants believe that the Bible is inerrant. It is no more reasonable to believe that the Bible is inerrant than to believe that the Pope is infallible.

When I started looking into it, I realized that the Bible is a collection of laws, letters, poetry, and stories, written by many different people in many different places at many different times. The Bible is filled with contradictions and errors, and it has been translated through many different cultural lenses, historical settings, and languages.

Also, the Bible contains accounts of events such as the great flood, which are similar to earlier pagan scriptures, and parables such as the prodigal son, which are similar to earlier Buddhist scriptures. If the Bible repeats or resembles a pagan or Buddhist scripture, is the earlier pagan or Buddhist scripture also inerrant or inspired by God?

Sadly, the Protestant church (like the Catholic church) expresses its beliefs firmly. Increasingly, we discover that there are contradictions and errors and myths in the Bible, which leads some Protestants to wonder, "What else is the church wrong about?"

Even if we think we know what the Bible says, it is difficult to know what it means, and many Christian readers find a metaphorical meaning in it, as do most non-Christians. In the East, Jesus is revered as a spiritual teacher, and he embodies the hero's journey. Jesus' story as metaphor may actually be more inspiring than his story as history.

JUSTIFICATION BY FAITH

Since the Reformation, Protestants believe that we are justified by faith in Jesus, and Paul mentions "faith in Jesus" in Romans 3:22, but some scholars believe that "faith in Jesus" should be translated as "faith of Jesus," analogous to the "faith of Abraham," wherein Abraham maintained enough trust in God to sacrifice his son.

If Paul really meant "faith of Jesus," as some scholars suggest, then this would warrant a major reworking of Christian theology.

For 500 years, there has been a dispute between Catholics, who believe (like James) that we are justified by faith and works, and Protestants, who believe (like Paul) that we are justified by faith. Jesus addressed this issue when he discussed how we are saved in Mark 10:19-21, and he never mentioned justification by faith:

> 19 "You know the commandments: 'You shall not murder; You shall not commit adultery; You shall not steal; You shall not bear false witness; You shall not defraud; Honor your father and mother.'"

(This sounds like "the law," which is very Jewish, or like "works," which is very Catholic.)

> 20 "He said to him, "Teacher, I have kept all these since my youth." 21 Jesus, looking at him, loved him and said, "You lack one thing; go, sell what you own, and give the money to the poor, and you will have treasure in heaven; then come, follow me."

(This sounds more difficult than "accepting Jesus Christ as your Lord and Savior," but the meaning is clear. Jesus never spoke about justification by faith in the synoptic gospels.)

There is a more essential problem with the popular notion of justification by faith. How is an assertion of belief any different than an act or a thought or a word (or a work?) If we are justified by our assertion, then are we saying that we are justified by our works? What looks like sensible theology to some looks like self-indulgent speculation to others.

What is left of Christianity without these speculations? Just Jesus.

CHAPTER 8

JESUS

Once, I googled "Christian values." At the time, the Wikipedia page mentioned three types of Christian values, including "conservative Christian values," such as opposition to abortion, and "liberal Christian values," such as inclusion of LGBTQ people. Interestingly, "Jesus' Christian values" were totally different from the other two types.

KINGDOM OF GOD

Jesus' primary teaching was to announce the Kingdom of God. At times, Jesus spoke about the Kingdom as if it had arrived. At other times, he spoke about it as if it would soon arrive, even in the lifetime of his listeners. That never happened, so early Christians, starting with the writers of the Gospels, projected a second coming in the future.

Some Christians conflate the Kingdom of God with the church or the community, but Jesus seemed to be referring to a new order in which human society is transformed. There is no "us and them" in the Kingdom. Everyone loves their neighbors, even their enemies.

Jesus was sent to the lost sheep of Israel, and he was kind to those who suffered from oppression, poverty, and sickness. Jesus contrasted the Kingdom with the Roman Empire, and he accepted the same laudatory titles that Caesar accepted for himself. Although Jesus never sought to overthrow the government, he was killed for sedition.

INCLUSION

Jesus was compassionate, and he had compassion for the rich, who would have difficulty being saved. Jesus was not opposed to power or wealth on premise, but he was opposed to their misuse, and he taught his followers to value the spiritual, not the material. He had compassion for friends and relatives, but also for strangers, such as the rich young man and the Samaritan woman and numerous disabled people and lepers.

ORTHOPRAXY

Jesus' message got lost in the shuffle. Nothing in the Nicene Creed derives from the words and works of Jesus, except for the statement "He was crucified under Pontius Pilate; he suffered, died and was buried"—and this is what was done to him, not what he did or said.

There is only a comma between the mention of Jesus' birth and death, supplanting any of the things that Jesus did or said, as if it is important to believe that Jesus is "begotten, not made" but not to believe that Jesus taught us to love our neighbors.

Every Sunday, Christians recite a creed that says nothing of Jesus' words or works. Instead, the creed engages in theological speculation (not revelation) largely based on Greek philosophy, other religions, and pagan practices.

THE GOLDEN RULE

Jesus was more concerned with orthopraxy or right action, than orthodoxy or right belief, and he did not develop a creed or any doctrines. He completed the law, but he did not add to it; he summarized the law as "Love God above all else, and love your neighbor as yourself." This is the Golden Rule, common to almost all traditions.

In its weak form, the Golden Rule suggests that we treat others as we were treated, regardless of any differences in our circumstances. In its strong form, the Golden Rule suggests that we treat others as we were treated, after allowing for their differing circumstances.

HEALING

Jesus was a healer, and he saw acts of healing as harbingers of the Kingdom. Whenever he healed someone, he restored the person to wholeness and rewarded their faith.

He healed friends and relatives, but he also healed Gentiles and Romans. He taught that God is impartial, that God sends rain on the just and the unjust. In that light, we should probably think twice before we declare that we are "chosen" or "saved."

TEACHING

Jesus was a teacher who challenged those who honored the letter, rather than the spirit, of the law. He spoke in parables, which required his listener to draw his or her own conclusions, and his stories often illustrated that God's ways are different than our ways.

Some of Jesus' sayings and stories are repeated in other places and times, and some of the sayings attributed to Jesus may have actually been spoken by other people. Still, Jesus' wisdom is consistent with other great spiritual teachers in other traditions.

WHOLENESS

Jesus was a uniter. He was interested in the good of the many, not just the few, and he cared for all of mankind, not just for his fellow Jews or his followers. He was radically inclusive, ministering to foreigners, sinners, slaves, and tax collectors. There were women among his followers, and women served as deacons in the community.

Jesus cared about wholeness, rather than holiness. Although Christians sometimes aspire to greatness or perfection, Jesus was comfortable with weakness and imperfection.

Although some Christians view grace as the foundation of Christian beliefs and practices, Jesus never even mentioned grace. Why would Jesus omit such an "important" teaching, and why would Paul emphasize it, if Jesus never even mentioned it?

TRANSFORMATION

Jesus did not seek to found a religion, and he would not recognize a modern church service. Tradition tells us that Thomas, one of the twelve apostles, evangelized in India. Today, Indian Christians with apostolic roots refer to Jesus as "Eeesho," which was his name in Aramaic. No doubt, there are other ancient Christian conventions, like this one, that have long been forgotten.

Jesus focused on God, not himself, and he gave God credit for his words and works. Near the end of his ministry, he said that his followers were his friends, not his servants, and that he wanted them to enjoy the relationship with God that Jesus enjoyed. This involves transformation, accepting a new way of life, not simply adopting a new set of beliefs.

Generally, the words and works of Jesus conform to the perennial philosophy that seeks the common truth in all traditions. Although there are passages in the gospels that seem to reflect the views of the writers, rather than the views of Jesus, the picture that emerges places Jesus among the great teachers in the many traditions across all of time.

Imagine that the creed encouraged us to love our neighbors as ourselves and to turn the other cheek, or that the creed restated portions of the parables and the Sermon on the Mount. Would such a creed be more inspiring, more life-affirming, and more practical?

CHAPTER 9

THE CONTEMPORARY CHRISTIANS

Christianity today is different than Jewish Christianity in Jesus' day. Christianity, like many religions, was originally called The Way, but what began as a transformative way of life became a rigid system of beliefs.

HEAVEN AND HELL

Where Jesus said a lot about the Kingdom of God and a little about the afterlife (and what he said about the afterlife was ambiguous) contemporary Christianity is preoccupied with the afterlife.

Bart D. Ehrman, a New Testament scholar, writes:

> To put it succinctly, the founders of Christianity did not believe that the soul of a person who died would go to heaven or hell.... There is no place for eternal punishment in any passage of the entire Old Testament. In fact—and this comes as a surprise to many people—nowhere in the entire Hebrew Bible is there any discussion at all of heaven and hell as places of rewards and punishments.

Ehrman considers Jesus' words, and he wonders whether Jesus was talking about:

- our collective fate or our individual fates, or

- the extinction of life or eternal conscious torment, or

- eternal conscious torment or temporary purgation, or

- an eternal soul or a physical resurrection.

He also wonders how a disembodied soul can be tormented.

There are serious practical questions concerning the notion of heaven and hell. How is our soul related to our body and brain? If our soul is not our body and brain or our personality and thoughts, what is it, and how does it go anywhere? Where does it go?

Some people think that vivid near-death experiences are proof of an afterlife. If we experience a bright light or a long tunnel in the process of our death, does that mean that there is no death, or that there is a bright light and a long tunnel just prior to death?

God is seen as a means to an end, if one is more concerned with having eternal life than with having a relationship with God. Eternal life, too, can be a means to an end, if one is more concerned that life is fair (or suitably rewarded) than that life is lived well, with love for others.

Paul Tillich, a Christian philosopher, discussed eternal life in terms that sound more Eastern than Western, saying, "The New Testament speaks of eternal life, and eternal life is not continuation of life after death. Eternal life is beyond past, present, and future: we come from it, we live in its presence, we return to it."

As atheist Ludwig Feuerbach wrote, "If there is not another and a better life, God is not just and good. The justice and goodness of God are thus made dependent on the perpetuity of individuals," recognizing this false link between eternal life and justice.

Mystic Cynthia Bourgeault writes that "Our earthly existence, then, is not about good behavior or final judgment. It's not a finishing school in which we 'learn what we need to learn,' nor a sweatshop in which we work off our karmic debt."

EXCLUSION

Where Jesus was radically inclusive, contemporary Christianity is radically exclusive. Most traditions emphasize oneness or unity, not duality or separation.

Since Genesis, Christianity has been based on the separation of God and humans, land and water, earth and sky, plants and animals, animals and humans, men and women. Jesus did not separate people. He loved Jew and Gentile, rich and poor, saint and sinner.

Later, the Christian churches distinguished between Christians and non-Christians, Catholics and non-Catholics, clergy and laity, straight people and LGBTQ people, etc. Again, Jesus likely never made these distinctions.

Also, Christianity has always had a difficult relationship with the other religions. The Catholic church sanctioned the Crusades and the Inquisition, as well as colonization and genocide. Many Christian churches approved of slavery, and some churches owned slaves themselves.

In World War II, many Christian churches sided with the Nazis, not against them. The Catholics signed a concordat with the Nazis, the Orthodox dedicated Mt. Athos to Hitler, and some of the Protestants in Germany aligned with Hitler and the Nazis.

Today, some Christians oppose practices such as abortion and same-sex marriage, but rather than refrain from these practices, they want to impose their beliefs on others. It is a belief, not a fact, that life begins at conception or that sexual orientation is a choice or that gender is binary or that "natural law" defines clear roles. In fact, some cultures recognize more than two genders.

Abortion is a complicated issue, and marriage protects essential rights. In a democratic, heterogeneous, secular society like ours, a minority cannot impose its will on those who do not share their beliefs, no matter how firmly they hold them, and they cannot claim to have a "free pass" to violate others' rights.

ORTHODOXY

Where Jesus was all about orthopraxy, contemporary Christianity is all about orthodoxy. Much Christian doctrine was developed many years after Jesus' death, and much Christian doctrine concerns belief, rather than practice. Most other traditions are more concerned with action and contemplation, rather than beliefs and creeds.

Thankfully, Jesus was not prone to speculation, so his words ring true to this day (even if some of the Christian doctrine, which was based on speculation, does not).

LIFE AND DEATH

Where Jesus taught us how to live, contemporary Christianity tells us how Jesus died. Many Christians have a difficult time squaring Jesus' tragic death with justice or mercy, and the doctrine of substitutionary atonement, which suggests that Jesus died for our sins, seems barbaric and nonsensical to many people.

Roger Wolsey, a progressive Christian minister, writes, "Jesus lived and died *for* us not *instead of* us. He didn't seek to live and die on our behalf as our 'proxy,' as our 'substitute.' He hoped to wake us up into realizing who we really are as God's children and embolden us so that we might truly live as God intends."

SUFFERING

Where Jesus tried to relieve suffering, contemporary Christianity glorifies suffering. Martyrs who died for their beliefs were revered by many in the early church. "Jesus suffered, he suffers with us, and suffering will be rewarded in the afterlife," say some Christians, but none of this helps us to relieve actual suffering in the here and now.

Contemporary Christianity rationalizes suffering, too. If I am wealthy, perhaps God intended it, and if I am poor, then perhaps God intended that, too. Would God prefer this world with a few billionaires and millions of poor people, or would God prefer a kinder world with fewer billionaires and fewer poor people?

SUPERFICIALITY

Where Jesus emphasized the spiritual, rather than the material, contemporary Christianity emphasizes the material. Many Christians believe that God blesses believers with prosperity and that a lack of prosperity signals a lack of belief or a lack of prayer.

Vivekananda, a Hindu sage, wrote, "Pray for knowledge and light; every other prayer is selfish." Much prayer consists of talking, not listening, and saying "please," not "thank you."

SUPERNATURALISM

Where Jesus was reluctant to perform miracles, contemporary Christianity embraces the supernatural aspects of Jesus' story, such as virgin birth, divine sonship, and physical resurrection.

Contemporary Christianity, especially Protestantism, was heavily influenced by Paul's writings. In 1 Corinthians 15:14, Paul wrote, "If Christ has not been raised, then our proclamation has been in vain and your faith has been in vain."

Similarly, author C.S. Lewis asserted that supernatural claims about Jesus presented a trilemma, suggesting that Jesus is either Lord, liar, or lunatic. Many modern readers view these hyperbolic challenges as false choices.

As more Christians question the personal nature of God and the supernatural claims about Jesus, theologian John D. Caputo poses a provocative question, asking, "Does the Kingdom of God need God?"

Imagine that Jesus was not born of a virgin; instead, he was conceived the normal way. In some ways, that is an even more powerful story.

Imagine that Jesus was not the second person of the Trinity; instead, he was of the same mind of God, but not of the same nature. In some ways, that is an even more powerful story.

Imagine that Jesus was not resurrected; instead, he appeared in visions to 500 people. In some ways, that is an even more powerful story.

If Jesus was born as a man, lived as a man, and died as a man (albeit a very special man), would any of us live our lives any differently?

If Jesus was not born of a virgin, if he was not divine, if he was not resurrected, would the wisdom of his words and the power of his works lose their allure, or would we follow a historical Jesus as gladly as we follow a mythological Jesus?

What is left of Christianity when we look for an experiential awareness of God, rather than an intellectual speculation about God? Enter the mystics, whom we will discuss shortly.

The Dark Night of the Soul

Before we discuss the mystics, we need to discuss a common experience for many on the spiritual path. John of the Cross wrote a lot about the dark night of the soul, which describes a period of desolation in which there is no consolation.

Once, I thought that the seeker loses the sense of God's presence during this time, but after experiencing a dark night of the soul myself, I now think that the seeker loses his or her concept of God, which is even more difficult in some ways.

Sylvia Salow, a spiritual life coach, writes, "The Dark Night of the Soul feels like a mini-death of our soul. When, in fact, it's a mini-death of our ego.... The Dark Night of the Soul isn't the end. It's the beginning. You're born again."

THE STAKES

When I began my journey, I expected to confirm my conventional Christian beliefs. I read everything that I could find on the beginnings of Christianity and its development over 2,000 years. As questions arose, I read everything that I could find to answer them.

Soon, I saw that a) Christian doctrine was premised on some assumptions, b) Christianity had not made allowances, in case any or all of these assumptions are false, and c) if one of these assumptions is false, then the rest of the doctrine might not hold up:

First, Christianity assumes that God is a personal God. If there is no personal god, then there would be no one to extend justice or mercy, no one to punish or reward us, and no point to living an eternal life.

Second, Christianity assumes that there is an afterlife. If there is no afterlife, there would be no point to judgment, no reason to extend justice or mercy, no punishment or reward for our behavior, and no distinction between believers and sinners.

Third, Christianity assumes that we have individuality, personhood, and a soul. If we do not have a soul, there would be no one to be judged, no one to accept justice or mercy, no one to collect punishment or reward, and no one to live an eternal life.

Fourth, Christianity assumes that we have free will. If we do not have free will, there would be no point to judgment, no basis for extending justice or mercy, no point to punishment or reward for our behavior, and no distinction between believers and sinners.

We cannot know whether there is a personal God or whether there is an afterlife, but science is beginning to suggest that our personhood is a construct and that there is no reason to believe that we have free will (and good reasons to believe that we do not).

Deconstruction can be very disconcerting (at first), when we ask the big questions. In some ways, it is more comforting to suppose that there is a God, that God has intention, that humans have souls, and that human souls outlive human bodies—but are all of these suppositions true?

What do the mystics say about God? What do the scientists say about the universe? Both seek truth through experience. What do the Eastern religions say about life? They seek truth through examining life as it is, not as we want it to be. As Lao Tzu said, knowledge through realization of the true state of life cannot cause harm.

LOSS

When we realize that our worldview is not as secure as we thought it was, there is a sense of loss—and if we lose our image of God and our image of ourselves, then it is a profound loss indeed.

The loss of a belief is like the loss of a friend, and the stages of grief are similar: denial, anger, bargaining, depression, and acceptance.

At this point, you might be thinking that this has been a very interesting, but very troubling, book. You might feel some anger, denial, or sorrow, and you might try to rationalize or reconcile your beliefs. I understand, because that is how I felt when I began to question my beliefs.

Eventually, I came to accept many of these facts and findings, but that did not come easily or quickly. Along the way, it was helpful to see glimmers of hope suggesting that there may be a belief system that makes better sense of the big questions I was facing about the physical and metaphysical worlds.

ANGER

Once I began to see that some of my beliefs were not supportable, I became angry with those who presented these beliefs to me as facts, without doing the homework to know if they were supportable or not and without presenting any caveats or contexts.

Also, I became angry with my Christian family members and friends, who tried to evangelize me without realizing that I had done the homework, that they had not, and that I likely knew more than they did about the tradition they were promoting.

Finally, I became angry that many contemporary Christian beliefs had strayed far from the words and works of Jesus. In doing so, many Christian churches had been unkind to divorced people, LGBTQ people, and non-Christian people, to name a few—and they had done it in the name of religion. Sadly, I had, too, for much of my life.

Some Christian beliefs have led to a type of passivity among Christians, whereby it is easier for some Catholics to confess their sins to a priest than to truly repent, and for some Protestants to "accept Jesus as your Lord and Savior" than to truly transform themselves.

Worse, for some Protestants, good behavior sounds a lot like "works," and some Protestants are less likely to do good works because of that association.

In the same vein, some Christians are discouraged from following Jesus' example because they think that Jesus is God and they are not. If Jesus is thought to be an example, rather than an exception, then his words and works become really compelling.

Some Christians do not feel compelled to take care of the planet or their fellow humans because they think that Jesus is coming soon and that he will set things right then.

Some Christians use their beliefs as reasons not to help others. They might say that "Charity breeds dependency" or "Jesus said that the poor will always be with us" or "Jesus might want someone else to help" or "The church will help."

If we take Jesus seriously, then we have pretty high expectations of Christians and very high expectations of ourselves, and we can get angry when it seems like Jesus' words or works are being ignored or misunderstood.

DISCERNMENT

There have been some saints and sages throughout history who addressed the big questions, and we can learn a lot from them. There have been some crackpots and hucksters too, and we need to be able to distinguish between the saints and the hucksters.

It is not helpful to deconstruct our beliefs, without also reconstructing our beliefs. At the same time, it is not helpful to deconstruct an unwieldy belief system, only to reconstruct an equally unwieldy belief system in its place.

Comments and Responses

When people find out that I am on a spiritual journey and that I am writing a book, they can feel threatened, as if I am challenging their beliefs when I challenge my own. There are a few conversations that I have had several times, so I will recount them here.

"If I have to examine everything that I was ever taught, that will take a lot of work."

Agreed. I had to read 1,000 books and spend 20 years reflecting and researching before I could write this book. Hopefully, the book saves you some time and provides you with some questions to explore on your own.

"A lot of this information is new to me. Why am I hearing a lot of this for the first time?"

That is a great question. I think that many people do not ask difficult questions about their beliefs because they prefer certainty and comfort to uncertainty and discomfort.

Many people (sadly) "throw out the baby with the bathwater," and reject Jesus because they do not believe in global floods, talking snakes, and virgin births. We can follow Jesus without accepting supernatural claims.

On his deathbed, Buddha was reported to have instructed his followers not to accept anything without confirming it themselves, even Buddha's own words. If anything in this book seems uncertain or uncomfortable to you, then you should confirm it yourself.

"It seems like you are a 'cafeteria' Christian, picking and choosing your beliefs."

All Christians are cafeteria Christians. Maybe you believe in original sin or the Trinity—these doctrines are not in the Bible. Maybe you believe that we are saved by grace—Jesus never said anything about grace.

Maybe you believe in the virgin birth or the physical resurrection—these doctrines are in later books of the Bible, not in earlier ones. Maybe you believe that the Pope is infallible, a recent Catholic theory, or that the Bible is inerrant, a recent Protestant theory.

Are you a cafeteria Christian?

**"You question some well-accepted beliefs.
What proof do you have?"**

I cannot prove that Jesus was not divine, that he was not born of a virgin, or that he was not resurrected from the dead. No one else can prove that he was any of these things.

Years ago, people used to believe that Zeus was born of a goddess and a Titan, that he flooded the earth to punish humanity, and that he killed people with thunderbolts. Thunder was seen as proof that Zeus existed, as there was no other explanation for it at the time. I cannot prove that Zeus did not exist, and no one else can prove that he did.

**"If my beliefs are not supportable,
then I would rather not even know about it."**

My journey gave me valuable perspective about how to live my life right. The consequences of living my life wrong can be pretty serious.

If Jesus is not God—and he only said that his way was God's way—then are we idolaters if we worship Jesus as God? At the same time, if we lay awake worrying about being smited by all of the gods that we do not worship, will we ever get any sleep?

**"I only read one book [meaning the Bible] but
it is a really good book."**

Agreed. I read that book many times, and I like it too. I understand how some people read the book literally and how others read it allegorically, metaphorically, or mythically.

Also, I learned a lot about interpretations, based on the cultures, languages, and people that wrote the book, and I learned about how the book was interpreted over time.

"I am too humble to believe that God is in everyone and everything. I am not God."

Humility is good, and no one is suggesting we are each the creators of the universe. The idea that "God is in everyone and everything" requires a different understanding of God, namely that God is the "ground of being" (as Tillich said) rather than a being itself. Certainly, if we think of God as a person, then we are not God, and God is not us.

Some people who are too humble to believe that God is in them are not too humble to believe that they have a personal relationship with the creator of the universe. Atheist Christopher Hitchens asks, "How much vanity must be concealed—not too effectively at that—in order to pretend that one is the personal object of a divine plan?"

"I am too humble to think that I am as smart as Saint Augustine and 2,000 years of history."

Augustine was a smart person, and I read many of his writings. I do not claim to be smarter than him, but we all have the benefit of 1,600 years of history, philosophy, and science, as well as the reactions to Augustine by others who were as smart as him. Would Augustine write the same books if he knew what we know now?

Augustine might have been inspired by God, but not all of his works have stood the test of time. For example, Augustine wrote, "Woman does not possess the image of God herself but only when taken together with the male who is her head, so that the whole substance is one image."

"I am a follower of Jesus, and nothing you can say will shake my beliefs."

I am a follower of Jesus, too. As a matter of fact, I was so inspired by Jesus' story of the rich young man that I quit my job and sold my house to spend my life in service to others. I take Jesus at least as seriously as anyone else—maybe even more so.

Also, I have not been critical of Jesus, although I may have been critical about Christian doctrine that Jesus did not originate, and I may have questioned beliefs about Jesus that Jesus did not profess.

"This all seems very intellectual and impractical to me. What difference does it make?"

Perhaps some of these discussions are intellectual, but they are not impractical. When we learn about the mystics, their testimony is experiential, not intellectual, and when we learn about the scientists, their testimony is certainly practical. Would we live different lives if we truly realized our interconnectedness?

Spirituality is supposed to transform people, and throughout the rest of this book, we will discuss how I was transformed from a materialistic and selfish religious person to an open-hearted and open-minded spiritual person. After questioning my politics, my religion, and my personality, I became a better person who lives a better life.

All theology is speculation, but it has teeth. Good theology breeds good behavior, and bad theology breeds bad behavior. I lived my life very differently once I discovered that everyone is related, and everything is connected.

PART 2

RECONSTRUCTION

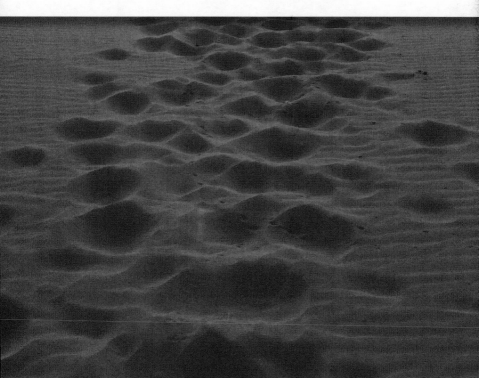

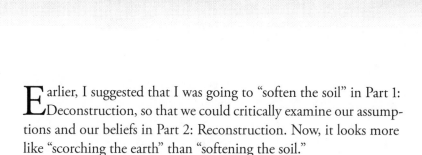

Earlier, I suggested that I was going to "soften the soil" in Part 1: Deconstruction, so that we could critically examine our assumptions and our beliefs in Part 2: Reconstruction. Now, it looks more like "scorching the earth" than "softening the soil."

SCORCHING THE EARTH

I realized that creation myths and divine sonship and physical resurrections and virgin births were features of many ancient religions.

I realized that concepts such as creation *ex nihilo* (out of nothing) and linear time (having a beginning and an end) and Newtonian physics (matter as objects) were Western concepts, not universal concepts, and that not all cultures view the world this way.

I realized that dualistic concepts such as good or evil, heaven or hell, and angels or devils were Zoroastrian concepts and that many modern Zoroastrians view these concepts allegorically, metaphorically, or mythically, not literally.

I realized that events such as the creation and the exodus and the global flood, as well as people such as Abraham and Moses and Noah were Jewish innovations, and that many modern Jews viewed these events and people as mythology, not history.

I realized that concepts such as original sin and the Trinity and substitutionary atonement were theories invented by humans, not absolute Truths revealed by God.

I realized that concepts such as Lord and Messiah and Son of God and Son of Man were honorific terms, but not divine terms, and that in Jesus' time they would not indicate divinity.

I realized that the modern church traces its beginnings to the Council of Nicaea, where all of these imported and interpreted concepts were decreed as orthodoxy by the Catholic bishops, not by Jesus or James or the apostles or the earliest Christians.

SOFTENING THE SOIL

Jesus did not talk about doctrine, so we can disagree with Augustine about original sin or with Tertullian about the Trinity or with Anselm about substitutionary atonement, without disagreeing with Jesus.

You might be wondering (as I was) why we have not heard any of this before. The simple answer is that we never asked, and our parents and priests never asked either.

Those who support these beliefs are mostly apologists, who reject any spirituality that does not conform with their own beliefs. Those who oppose these beliefs are mostly materialists, who reject any spirituality at all. Few of them are seeking truth in any universal sense.

Perhaps we can reconstruct a philosophy, a theology, and a worldview that agrees with the words and works of Jesus, while comporting with what we know about the universe.

We will now look at alternative worldviews, as described by the mystics of all religions (including Christianity), by the saints and sages of Eastern religions (including Buddhism, Hinduism, and Taoism), and by the scientists (including the quantum physicists).

During my reconstruction, I baked in a sweat lodge, chanted to Shiva, meditated in a zendo, and whirled with the dervishes. In my opinion, I am now following Jesus more closely than ever, and my spirituality is deeper, fuller, and richer than ever—thanks to the Eastern religions, the mystics, and the scientists.

Vanaprastha
(The Forest Dweller)

During the third stage of life, a person renounces material pursuits and retires to the forest, pursuing a life of contemplation and service.

MIDLIFE CRISIS

In midlife, I discovered a deepening disconnect between the person I was and the person I knew I should be. I had a patient wife who was quickly losing patience, and two young children who were rapidly growing up without me.

At work, I no longer liked, respected, or trusted some of the people that I worked for or (worse) the person that I had become. I acquired a cardiologist, a marriage counselor, and a psychiatrist.

My patient wife politely but pointedly told me, "I can live like this for a short while, but I feel like I have already been living like this for a long while." She saved me, by prodding me to take a good, hard look at the life that I was living, a life of cutthroat behavior, intense competition, material acquisition, and serious stress.

I took a swan dive from my corner office, leaving behind the big job and the big paycheck for parts unknown. This was probably the most courageous (and also the most cowardly) thing that I ever did. I acted from conviction (and desperation), and I promised myself that I would never lose myself again and that I would restore balance to my life.

THE GRAY-HAIRED GUY

I freelanced as a "fixer for hire," and I soon acquired clients and built a reputation. One day I saw a good friend, who had left the company that I had just left to start his own investment banking company.

He was acquiring clients and building a reputation even faster than I was, and he made a plea for help, saying, "My company is too big for me to handle, and I need someone I trust," he said. "You are the only one I trust."

My wife was not pleased to hear that I was returning to the public finance arena. "What exactly is your role?" she asked. "Are you the relationship guy or the technical guy or the workhorse?" Not exactly. "Oh no," she said, "are you the gray-haired guy?" Exactly.

Over the next 15 years, I did my best work, financing a lot of schools and streets and sewers, and also a lot of airports, colleges, hospitals, sports facilities, and toll roads.

THE RICH YOUNG MAN

In the Bible, there is a haunting story about a rich young man who cannot bring himself to sell his possessions, give to the poor, and follow Jesus. I saw myself in that man, and I wondered whether my house or my job were as important to me.

This is not a Christian idea; it is a universal idea. Show me your guru or monk or mullah or rabbi, and I will show you an Arabic or Hebrew or Pali or Sanskrit text about dying to self. In plain English, as pastor Rick Warren says, "It's not about you."

If you live in the same neighborhood, pick your kids up at the same schools, shop in the same stores, and worship in the same churches for many years, then you constantly see the same people. They probably act like you, look like you, and think like you.

If you serve a wider community, then you see a wide variety of people who are all ages, races, and sexual orientations—and they may not act like you, look like you, or think like you. The more different people you meet, the more you realize we are all connected, and we are all related.

When Ramana Maharshi, a Hindu sage, was asked, "How are we to treat others?" he replied, "There are no others." When we serve other people and share their burdens, we develop empathy—which is much more compassionate than sympathy. Their joys are our joys, and their sorrows are our sorrows.

—

In my fifties, I realized that my karma bank was overdrawn, that I had taken much more than I had given, and that I could count on one hand the times that I had helped others, except for the times that I was expected to do so or that I was paid to do so.

Once again, I left behind the big job and the big paycheck. We moved from a 4,000-square-foot house to a 1,600-square-foot condominium, determined to spend the rest of our lives in service to others.

SAN ANTONIO, TEXAS

In 2013, we moved to San Antonio for a year. We moved half of our stuff, rented an apartment, and took care of our grandson.

We dropped everything that we were doing, and spent our time changing and feeding him, napping, and playing. We saw his first steps and his first words, and we watched him discover that he was a person. (He will have to unlearn that important, but incomplete, lesson.)

Our grandson taught us to love unconditionally, and our other two grandsons taught us again. As grandparents, we were responsible for them in the here and now, but we were not responsible as their parents were, worrying about their future choices and their future happiness. We could simply enjoy every minute with them, and we did.

We knew that our love for our grandsons had nothing to do with their appearances, behaviors, personalities, or responses to us. We would have loved them if they were adopted, if they were orphans or refugees. We realized that we should love everyone like we loved our grandsons.

HOHOE, GHANA

For five weeks, Jill and I went to Hohoe, a small village in West Africa, to teach. We lived in a dormitory with other volunteers, and we lived much like Ghanaians lived, with erratic electricity, leaky plumbing, no air conditioning, and no paved roads.

Despite their poverty, the people were generous and optimistic. They were religious, too, and there were exuberant church services.

Some Christians believe that we can manifest our own prosperity. In Africa and elsewhere, despite abiding faith and fervent prayers, many people cannot manifest their own prosperity.

We should all be grateful, whether we are "blessed" or not—and if we are blessed, we should not assume that we are favored. God causes his sun to rise on the evil and the good, and sends his rain on the righteous and the unrighteous. God is not partial.

We forget that we live in a world where the average person makes less than $2 a day. Without food, clothing, shelter, education, health care, and opportunity, how could someone manifest prosperity?

More important, if we say that God has blessed us with abundance because he loves us, what are we saying about those whom God has not blessed with abundance?

After our time in Ghana, we were haunted by the question, "Now that you know, what will you do?" *Do we send a computer?* They do not have electricity. *Do we send a generator?* They do not have fuel. *Do we first provide indoor plumbing?*

After we returned home, we began helping several young African men and women to pay for their college educations. We have paid for six degrees already, and we hope to pay for several more in the coming years. This may be the most important thing we ever did.

There are two moments in each relationship that can bring me to tears—one is when the students see that their lives are changing forever and the other is when the students send us their graduation pictures.

ACCRA, GHANA

My wife, Jill, got a bug bite that became infected, and she received intravenous antibiotics in a primitive, poorly-equipped hospital for four days. We went to the hospital with only a bottle of water and $24 in cash. The banks there did not recognize our credit cards.

Our host transported us, other volunteers loaned us $400, our insurance company arranged for Jill's care, and she fully recovered. Afterward, I had a humbling epiphany on a street corner of Accra, the capital city.

I told our host that this could not happen again. I had never been alone, in a foreign country, in trouble, without resources, unable to pay my way or talk my way or think my way out of a tough spot. "Send lawyers, guns, and money!" as singer Warren Zevon pleaded.

"Help me to understand," our host said. "Your wife is well. You are going back to Hohoe, where you have food, housing, and transportation. Your friends lent you $400, and you might be the only person in Accra with $400 in cash. What is the problem?"

I was filled with regret and shame. I had a humbling epiphany on that street corner in Accra, and I vowed that if I am ever tested again, I will trust in myself and others and God (or fate or the Universe) and NOT in the mistaken belief that I can control things.

Ten years later, we were tested again, while vacationing in Ecuador. We were quarantined with COVID for ten days in a small hotel room. Recalling our experience in Ghana, we were able to handle this emergency with much more equanimity.

ALBANY, NEW YORK

In 2013, a friend of mine had a serious illness. We had known each other for a long time, but not well, and she once posted a statement on social media that said something like, "The worst part of being strong is that no one ever asks if you're okay."

Most people do not know what to do in this situation, and all that we can do is to reach out. We started texting, then calling, then visiting, and we enjoyed getting to know each other.

We talked about everyday stuff, like our children and grandchildren, but we talked about serious stuff too. People who are dying are usually really authentic, and people who reach out to them should be too.

When she died, I had a hard cry, and I still think about her. Since then, I reach out to people who are suffering, because I know that accompanying others in their suffering enriches all of our lives.

VA OUTPATIENT CLINIC

Since 2011, I have been driving a van for the Veterans Administration, transporting veterans to doctors' appointments. Many are blind or disabled, and some do not have cars. Some appear able-bodied, but if you spend time with them, you realize that they have narcolepsy or PTSD or another unseen disability that prevents them from driving.

Before I drove, I did not see people with disabilities. I might not notice a person in a wheelchair. I might let a door slam on a person with a walker. I might let a person with a cane struggle across the street. I might try to help a disabled person, whether they asked for help or not. After I drove, I knew better.

A friend told me that a van driver is like a ferryman of souls, carrying precious cargo—passengers, not packages. Going to the homeless shelter? Released from prison? Struggling with PTSD? Hop in.

One day, I was asked to pick up a new veteran who was a registered sex offender. *I didn't sign up for this,* I thought. *Should I pick him up? Should*

I even speak to him? What exactly did I sign up for? I asked myself. "You signed up to drive folks to the VA." Hop in.

I recalled the conversation between Arjuna and Krishna in the *Bhagavad Gita*, when Arjuna said that he did not want to fight. Krishna asked him about his profession. When Arjuna said that he was a warrior, Krishna said that he should certainly fight because that was his purpose.

As spiritual teacher Ram Dass said, "We're all just walking each other home." When we realize that this is the highest and best use of our lives, then our purpose becomes helping others, rather than judging them.

AMERICAN ASSOCIATION OF RETIRED PEOPLE (AARP) FOUNDATION AND VOLUNTEER INCOME TAX ASSISTANCE (VITA)

Since 2012, I have been volunteering for AARP and VITA, helping low- and moderate-income families to file their federal taxes, and I prepared more than 1,000 tax returns. Of course, taxes are very personal, and you can learn a lot about a person in 30 seconds:

> This is my W-2. I made a lot of money until I got laid off.

> This is my 1099-MISC. After I got laid off, I worked construction.

> This is my 1099-G. After my savings ran out, I collected unemployment.

> This is my 1099-R. After my bills piled up, I cashed out my retirement savings.

Sadly, this is a common story. The Federal Reserve Board says that half of all Americans cannot find $400 in an emergency. People with jobs may not have secure jobs, and even people with secure jobs may live paycheck to paycheck.

Many employers do not offer health insurance or retirement benefits, and many employees cannot afford to contribute to health insurance or retirement savings anyway. Many people work as contractors, they do not work regularly, they do not get benefits, and they pay their own income taxes and self-employment taxes.

At one site where I volunteer, many of the taxpayers are immigrants, including some who are documented and some who are not. It might surprise people to learn that undocumented immigrants pay taxes, but they do, and many work several jobs.

When you spend time with low- and moderate-income people, you realize that they are just like you and me. There is no need to demonize or lionize the poor—or the rich.

Whether we are rich has as much to do with chance and circumstance as with choice and character. Was I "rich" because I worked harder or had better luck? Yes, and yes. Some poor folks underestimate the importance of effort; some rich folks underestimate the importance of luck.

When I was among the one percent, I used to think that there were makers and takers, that the makers (us) worked and paid taxes, while the takers (them) loafed and took benefits. Then, I met an undocumented immigrant working three part-time jobs with no benefits, and a working mother choosing between paying rent or paying insurance.

It is one thing to embrace free markets. It is another thing to support public policies and tax reforms that take from the poor and give to the rich. Overall, I paid more than $1 million in federal income taxes, and I never resented it, because my taxes paid for the courts and hospitals and roads and schools that helped me to succeed.

There are places in the world that lack the services that are essential to success, and there are places in the USA that do, too.

AMERICAN RED CROSS

I spent a few years volunteering on the Disaster Action Team for the American Red Cross, where I responded to local emergencies, providing food, clothing, and shelter for people displaced by fires, floods, hurricanes, and tornadoes.

Although the Red Cross cannot replace a house or permanently relocate a family, it can provide temporary assistance when a family is in crisis. In addition to providing food, clothing, and shelter, it can provide transitional assistance.

Many families live on the edge, so if their homes burn down, they may not have insurance. They may not have bank accounts, so they may lose their cash, too. Despite their hardships, these families showed courage and resourcefulness, and we were humbled to stand with them on the worst days of their lives.

CAMP JOHN MARC

Every week for a few years, I played with sick children at Cook Children's Medical Center. Also, I spent a few weeks as a camp counselor at Camp John Marc, an overnight camp for children with serious illnesses and disabilities, such as cancer and muscular dystrophy.

Many of the children would never experience archery, horseback riding, or swimming without the accommodations the camp provided. There were doctors, nurses, and pharmacists onsite, so the children received the care they needed.

Camp also provided opportunities for the children to share their experiences and to face their concerns and fears. Those with fatal illnesses, such as muscular dystrophy, accepted that they might have short lives and years of rapidly declining health. Those with treatable illnesses, such as cancer, worried about whether they would be cured, and whether they would get sick again after they were cured.

The camp also hosted the siblings of children with serious illnesses and injuries, and often they had fears of their own. I will never forget a girl whose brother died. "God spoke to me," she said. "He said that he took my brother because he loved my brother, and that he took my brother to a better place." I do not know if God spoke to her, but I suspect that if God spoke to her, then God would have said something like that.

TARRANT COUNTY HOMELESS COALITION

For a few years, I participated in the annual homeless count. Volunteers, often accompanied by police officers and service providers, visit homeless camps and shelters to survey the homeless people and provide emergency services.

There are homeless people living in almost every community. They live in or near populous and well-traveled areas, camping in the woods or living behind restaurants or underneath bridges. Some homeless people arrange with landlords to provide security in exchange for shelter.

There are many reasons why someone might be homeless, including domestic abuse, mental illness, and unemployment. Sometimes, they are suddenly and temporarily homeless, and there are an alarming number of homeless women and children.

Some people are homeless by choice. Regardless, it is difficult to escape homelessness, since homeless people may not have addresses, identification, or phones. Also, they may not have access to clothing or health care, or shower and toilet facilities.

———

After volunteering for ten years, I transformed from a single-minded investment banker to an open-hearted and open-minded spiritual seeker. My life was richer. I had more friends and deeper friendships. I cried more, and I laughed more. I connected with people naturally, without regard to whether they were "useful" to me.

Also, I grew to understand love differently, seeing that liking and loving are two different things. When we like someone, it is personal; it has something to do with uniqueness, such as appearance or character or intellect. Liking is conditional. When we love someone, it is impersonal; it has nothing to do with uniqueness. Loving is unconditional.

My politics changed, and my spirituality changed, too, after meeting disabled people, homeless people, mentally ill people, poor people, sick people, undocumented immigrants, and unemployed people. I knew their stories. I knew that everyone is related, and everything is connected. I valued each of them as human beings.

CHAPTER 10

THE MYSTICS

A mystic is a person who seeks union with God or unity with the Universe through contemplation and self-surrender. Every tradition, including Christianity, has its mystics, but Christianity is generally more doctrinal and less mystical than other traditions.

The mystics, even those who believe in a personal God, often experience God as a great darkness or a great light, a great silence or a great sound, a great presence or a great void. Most perceive unity, where God permeates everyone and everything.

As Meister Eckhart, a Christian mystic, wrote, "Theologians may quarrel, but the mystics of the world speak the same language." Though our concepts of God are unique, our experiences of God are similar, often remarkably so.

In *Theology Without Walls,* philosopher Richard Oxenberg writes:

> But many of us—more and more of us—have sensed, or intuited, or directly experienced that at the level of encounter, the level of *first-order knowledge,* there are similarities, complementarities, and correspondences between the spiritual state one enters when one feels oneself in touch with the God of Abraham and the spiritual state of the Hindu bhakti or the Buddhist arhat.

Mystical experiences may reveal an extraordinary reality that underlies ordinary life.

THE WAY OF THE HEART

Mysticism has an esoteric connotation, and it is sometimes errone-ously associated with the occult, so organized religion is often sus-picious of the mystics and their experiences. Several saints who are revered, such as John of the Cross, were initially tortured before they were ultimately canonized.

Catholicism has always been wary of mysticism, which seeks an unmediated path to God, and the church advises that anyone having a mystical experience should confirm it with a priest. Likewise, Prot-estantism is a religion more of the head than of the heart, and Mar-tin Luther preferred the "way of the cross" to the "way of the heart."

Most religions, including the Eastern Orthodox branch of Chris-tianity, embrace mysticism, and they seek a direct experience of God, regardless of their particular beliefs about God and unrestrained by their specific institutional structures.

PEAK EXPERIENCES

Drawing on classic studies by William James and F.C. Happold, as well as personal experience, philosopher Douglas W. Shrader explored seven characteristics of mystical experiences:

1. ineffability (the inability to capture the experience in ordi-nary language),

2. noetic quality (the notion that mystical experiences reveal an otherwise hidden or inaccessible knowledge),

3. transiency (the simple fact that mystical experiences last for a relatively brief period of time),

4. passivity (the sense that mystical experiences happen to someone; that they are somehow beyond the range of human volition and control),

5. unity of opposites (a sense of oneness, wholeness, or completeness),

6. timelessness (a sense that mystical experiences transcend time), and

7. a feeling that one has somehow encountered "the True Self" (a sense that mystical experiences reveal the nature of our true, cosmic self that is beyond life and death, beyond difference and duality, and beyond ego and selfishness).

These characteristics are strikingly common among those who seek union with God or unity with the Universe, and these commonalities are found across different traditions, in different places at different times—a Buddhist may experience enlightenment, a Christian may have ecstatic visions, and a Hindu may reach realization.

Symeon the New Theologian reported a "typical" mystical experience:

> a single divine ray shown right down on him and the room was full of light, and the young man….stayed there in ecstasy, forgot his individual self, and found no walls or roof over his head, because he saw light on every side…. He had no bodily cares or concerns of this world on his mind, but forgot the world and was wholly dissolved to become one with the divine light, so that it seemed to him that he was the light…. And so it was in truth that love and the desire he had for God took him out of the world in the spirit, and he forgot the world and the flesh and all the vain business of this life and was translated wholly into God.

William Blake, a mystic, related another mystical experience, writing, "To see the world in a grain of sand, and Heaven in a flower, hold infinity in the palm of your hand, and eternity in an hour."

Author David Carse describes a recent mystical experience in the Amazon jungle:

> In this part of that experience in the jungle, I knew three things about this Presence, about All That Is…. First, that

it is Alive. Not an inanimate cloud or energy field of some sort; nor even a thing which is alive: it is pure Life, Aliveness, Existence. Second, that this Presence is Intelligence. It is alert, awake, and Aware; it is Knowing. Not something that knows; rather it is the Knowing. Third, that its nature, its essence, is pure, unfathomable, endless, unconditional Love, Compassion, beauty, outpouring. In this Presence, I find myself in a state of overwhelming gratitude, bliss, unfathomable Peace, Love.

THE INDIVIDUAL

It is as interesting to note what the mystics DO NOT see as to note what they do see. Generally, the mystics of all traditions sense a presence, NOT a person. They sense a Oneness, NOT a cosmic rift between God and humans and NOT a judgment. They sense an immediacy in the here and now; they are NOT transported to heaven or hell.

When we review the common elements in mystical experiences over time, we have to ask why the typical mystical experience does not conform to Christian theology. If the mystics of all traditions encountered Jesus or heaven or a place of judgment, that would confirm the Christian ideas about God and afterlife and purpose.

Likewise, if the mystics of all traditions encountered the Great Spirit or Zeus, then that would confirm other traditions' ideas about God and afterlife and purpose. The typical mystical experience confirms an Eastern worldview, with an impersonal God, a presence in the here and now, and a sense of benevolence and connection.

THE UNIVERSAL

This experience is universal, and it has been reported in many different places and times, irrespective of whether someone is religious or what religion he or she practices, if any. It appears that when a Christian says "I found God" and a Buddhist says "I found the Void or emptiness," and a Hindu says "I found Brahman or fullness," they are essentially talking about the same experience.

Buddha's enlightenment under the bodhi tree likely was a mystical experience. Similarly, when Jacob Boehme saw the "foundations of things" in a pewter dish and when Julian of Norwich saw "all that is made" in a hazelnut and when William Blake saw the world in a grain of sand, they were all seeming to report mystical experiences.

THE PERSONAL

Although mystical experiences are impersonal, they are not cold or dispassionate. Any encounter with the divine, even an impersonal Universe, feels deeply personal.

In those rare instances where someone sees a person, rather than a presence, they often see the person that they most expect to see, so that a Hindu might see Krishna or a Catholic might see Mary. Maybe these are personal projections of impersonal perceptions, where someone overlays their individual conditioning upon a universal experience.

Many people have mystical experiences without recognizing them because they expect God to look or act a certain way, consistent with their culture and tradition.

Imagine that God appeared to you as the elephant-headed Hindu god, Ganesh. Would you say that God appeared to you, or would you say that you had a strange dream?

CHAPTER 11

TRANSCENDENCE

SCIENTIFIC DISCOVERIES

Studies show that almost one-third of us have had transcendent experiences. Huston Smith, an expert on comparative religions, believes that mystical experiences are the pinnacle of human consciousness. Scientists have studied the brain waves of mystics, noting an increase in delta and theta waves, which signal connection and creativity.

Scientists have observed that brain stimulation, hallucinogens, seizures, and strokes can produce experiences that are similar to mystical experiences. These events, like meditation and prayer, seem to remove filters that otherwise block the transcendent experience. Without these filters, we might be overwhelmed by every blade of grass and drop of dew.

Jill Bolte Taylor, a neuroscientist, experienced a stroke in the left side of her brain. (The left brain is analytical and logical, whereas the right brain is creative and intuitive.) She was unable to walk, talk, read, write, or recall her life. As she was losing her capacity, she had a mystical experience, and she was able to write about it after she recovered.

MEDITATION

Although a mystical experience can come upon a person at any time in any place, many people encounter God through meditation or prayer. Most Christians associate prayer with petitions, where we ask God for something, but this is the lowest form of prayer.

Joel S. Goldsmith, a spiritual teacher, wrote, "The only real gratitude is that which is felt for spiritual discernment. All else is thankfulness for things." Beyond petitionary prayer, centering prayer is Christian prayer that is like meditation, but it is not practiced widely.

One distinction between meditation and prayer is that meditation assumes an impersonal God and prayer assumes a personal God. If God is a field or a force or a presence, rather than a person, then we might enjoy a sense of connection and relatedness, as in a mystical experience, but we might be less likely to imagine a conversation or a relationship.

There are many types of meditation, and they generally fall under three categories:

- attention or concentration – the meditator chants a mantra (a sacred sound or word, often repeated silently) or concentrates on the breath or an external focus

- mindfulness or watching – the meditator allows thoughts to pass without becoming attached to them, sometimes using a mantra to return to watching thoughts

- silence or stillness – the meditator empties the mind of all thoughts, sometimes using a mantra to return to stillness

Some meditators believe that attention meditation is preparation for silent meditation, since we need to realize how we can focus in order to realize how we can relax our focus. Many traditions use repetition—chants, dance, prayer—to calm the "monkey mind" of unfocused thoughts and to clear the mind for awareness.

ENLIGHTENMENT

Awakening or enlightenment or realization is an experience of realizing the nature of the Self and of the Universe. When we realize that we are a part of the world, not apart from the world, then we see that we are woven into the fabric of the Universe. Most spiritual practitioners believe that awakening or enlightenment is a process.

In *The Sun Also Rises,* one of author Ernest Hemingway's characters goes bankrupt, and he says that the process happened "Gradually and then suddenly," and enlightenment is similar. Like fruit on a tree, it ripens slowly, falls suddenly, then continues to ripen.

Some Buddhists call the first stage of enlightenment "stream entry," and most people who enter the stream can point to a peak experience when they "get wet," even if they continue to "get wetter," through many small openings or several large openings. In Buddhism, enlightenment can produce *nirvana* or the cessation of suffering.

In most traditions, there are several openings, corresponding to head and heart (generally): wisdom and compassion (Buddhist), or justice and mercy (Christian), or *jnani*/wisdom and *bhakta*/devotion (Hindu). Often, there is a third opening, where one practices wisdom and compassion in the world. Adyashanti, a teacher in the Zen tradition, refers to corresponding openings of the head, the heart, and the gut.

In Zen, there are three fruits of practice arising from *zazen* or seated meditation. The first is *joriki* or concentration—single-minded attention, presence in the here and now; the second is *kensho* or seeing into one's true nature—similar to entering the stream; and the third is what Zen teacher Ruben Habito calls "embodying the peerless way"—integrating the *kensho* realization of Oneness into our daily lives.

Sometimes the Buddhists say, "Before enlightenment, carry water and chop wood; after enlightenment, carry water and chop wood." Few of us can spend our lives in caves, and fewer of us would even want to do that. Enlightenment is supposed to be embodied.

Jack Kornfield, a Buddhist teacher, wrote *After the Ecstasy, the Laundry,* which explains that part of the enlightenment process is to maintain the boundless presence that we can experience beyond space and time in our everyday world within space and time.

THREE PERSPECTIVES

It can be helpful to consider consciousness through three different perspectives, whereby we can see things through different lenses:

- With a microscope, we are composed of matter—which is really energy—and space. There is no difference between my cells and yours. We are made of the same stuff.

- With the naked eye, we seem to be separate people, knocking each other like billiard balls. Religions like Christianity, which focus on this level, are concerned with morality.

- With a telescope, we see communities, not individuals, or planets, not towns. These seemingly separate beings are connected and related.

In some traditions, there is another, ultimate perspective. Imagine that you can pan all the way out until you have a "God's-eye view" and you can see everything in the Universe. On the one hand, there is fullness. Everything is there—all of the creation and destruction—light and sound and matter. At the same time, there is emptiness. Everything is nothing, just darkness and silence and space.

EVERYDAY MYSTICS

Many people have peak experiences, but some of us do not recognize them as such. The spiritual journey is both experiential and intellectual, since we need knowledge to process spiritual experience, and we need experience to actualize spiritual knowledge.

Most spiritual practitioners agree that the goal of spiritual practice is realization of our true natures and (ultimately) transformation of our lives. The goal is not to have a certain experience or to reach a certain state. Do you see that everyone is related, and everything is connected? Whether you glimpse a mystical experience or an altered state, do you act like a mystic, speak like a mystic, and think like a mystic?

Transformation is much more important than enlightenment or liberation or realization. It is both experiential and intellectual, so whether we experience enlightenment or whether we understand enlightenment, if it does not transform who we are and how we live our lives, then it is just an interesting experience or an insightful understanding.

What can we learn from other traditions? Enter the Eastern religions.

CHAPTER 12

THE EASTERN RELIGIONS

The Eastern religions, including Buddhism, Hinduism, and Taoism, reflect an Eastern worldview, rather than a Western worldview, and there are significant differences between the Eastern religions and the Western religions.

PERSONS

In the West, ideas about God have a lot to do with the concept of personhood. For example, in Christianity:

- God is a person (or three persons) and Jesus is the second person in the Trinity.
- God is transcendent, meaning that we are "apart" from God.
- Adam and Eve created a cosmic rift between God and humans (original sin).
- Jesus came to atone for human sin and to repair the cosmic rift.
- If we accept Jesus as our personal savior, then we will live in heaven forever.

In the East, ideas about God have little to do with the concept of personhood. For example, in Hinduism:

- *Brahman* (the One) is the universal divine in everyone and everything.

- *Atman* is the particular divine in each of us, and *Atman* is *Brahman*.

- *Brahman* is not a person. Avatars and deities are persons, forms of *Brahman*.

- God is immanent, meaning that God is "a part" of us, rather than "apart" from us.

- There can be no rift between God and humans, thus nothing to atone for.

- If we see God in everyone and everything, then we live mindfully, here and now.

Personhood is cultural. In some languages, there is no first person singular ("I" or "me") or no distinction between first person singular ("I" or "me") and first person plural ("we" or "us.")

In India, the term *namaste* is a common greeting—it means "The divinity in me recognizes the divinity in you." In Christianity, God is primarily immanent in Jesus.

Nisargadatta Maharaj, a Hindu sage, and others say, "You are That," referring to the oneness of the Universe and our connection to everyone and everything.

In Buddhism, there is no mention of God, and there is a different view of personhood. The egoic self is viewed as a construct, which is ephemeral, not eternal. True Self is "no-self," meaning that there is no individual identity, separate from the Universe.

ESSENCE

In the East, some believe in a soul, an essence that survives our death, and some do not. Belief in a soul is related to belief in a self. Some Hindus believe in an individual self, but many Buddhists do not. For Buddhists, if we are reborn, who or what is reborn?

The notion that we may share in a *collective* divinity or soul, but that we may not possess an *individual* identity or soul, has theological ramifications. If I am not my body and my brain or my personality and my thoughts, then precisely who or what is this "I"?

What is our essence, aside from the ephemeral identities that we construct? If we are reborn or reincarnated, what part of us does that, absent our bodies and brains or our personalities and thoughts?

For some in the East, our *Atman,* our particular divinity, does not reincarnate. Simply, we are merged into *Brahman,* stirred into the cosmic soup, stripped of our individuality.

For many in the West, this can be a really disturbing realization. "So, I won't live forever?" No, not as "you." "So, I won't see Grandma?" No, not as "Grandma." "So, what do we live for?" We live for today, the here and now. Take a deep breath, and enjoy your time here.

Recall that the mystics of all traditions encounter the divine in the here and now, like the Eastern worldview, not in heaven or hell at another place at another time.

THE UNIVERSE

In the East, many believe that the Universe is eternal, that there is no beginning and no end, and that the Universe undergoes a cycle of beginnings and endings.

The Big Bang theory neither proves nor disproves the Eastern or the Western worldview, but whether the Universe is created or eternal has theological implications. If the Universe is eternal, then the beginning is "a creation," not "the creation;" the end times are "an end time," not "the end times;" and Jesus' second coming is "a coming," not "the coming."

If the Universe is eternal, then God did not create the Universe. God is the Universe or God inhabits the Universe, whether God is coterminous with the Universe (pantheism) or whether God is larger than the Universe (panentheism).

In this worldview, "theism," the belief in a personal god, makes little sense, and "atheism," the disbelief in a personal god, makes more sense. However, atheists argue that disbelief in a personal god does not necessarily mean disbelief in an impersonal force, something larger than ourselves. People write books about atheist spirituality.

Robin Meyers, a progressive Christian minister and scholar, and others use terms like "nontheistic" or "post-theistic" to describe this view—which has become increasingly popular in the West, as fewer people believe in a personal god now.

ABSOLUTE AND RELATIVE

Swami Abhayananda, a Hindu sage, studied many religious traditions, both Eastern and Western, and realized that there is a binitarian or two-natured concept of God that is common to almost all of them.

First, there is an "absolute" aspect of God, beyond space and time. Ramakrishna, a mystic, said that this is God without name or form. Philosopher Paul Tillich might call this the "God above gods" or the "ground of being," and mystic Meister Eckhart might call this the "Godhead."

God as the ground of being is not personal. The late Thich Nhat Hanh, a Buddhist monk who was nominated for a Nobel Prize, might say that we cannot have a relationship with this God, just like we cannot have a relationship with the sea or the sun. God as the ground of being cannot be contained by descriptions. In the East, they say *Neti Neti*, which means "Not this, not that."

Second, there is a "relative" aspect of God, within space and time. Ramakrishna said that this is God with name and form. Eckhart and Tillich might say that we invent these gods as intermediaries to approach the God above gods or the Godhead more easily.

Gods with name and form are personal. Thich Nhat Hanh might say that you can have a relationship with this God, as some Christians believe they have a relationship with Jesus. Gods with name and form can be contained by descriptions, so they can be worshipped, but it is never easy to describe the indescribable.

The notion of a personal god raises troubling philosophical questions, such as theodicy, which is the question of how an all-knowing and loving God can permit evil. Skeptics say that either God is unaware of evil or that God is unable to prevent evil.

Skeptics wonder why a loving God would not show himself. Those like the deists—who think that God created the universe, then left it to evolve without any intervention—have difficulty explaining why God would become interested in us again, after remaining invisible (or practically invisible) for so long.

Recall that the mystics of all traditions encounter an impersonal force, like the Eastern worldview, not a personal god, like the Western worldview.

KARMA AND AHIMSA

In the East, the term *karma* means that our actions determine our futures. *Karma* emphasizes cause and effect and intention. To the extent that we have free will, we can act with mindfulness, in ways that conform to the way of the Universe, to reduce suffering.

The *Bhagavad Gita* is an influential part of the *Mahabharata*, an ancient epic poem. In the *Gita*, Krishna, serving as a charioteer, advises Arjuna, a warrior entering battle, "You have a right to perform your duties, but you are not entitled to the fruits of your actions. Never consider yourself to be the cause of the results of your activities, nor be attached to inaction."

This non-attachment to outcomes is a difficult teaching in the West, where many are concerned with outcomes, quick to take credit for their actions, and resolved to enjoy the fruits of their actions.

In the East, the term *ahimsa* means "nonviolence." Some traditions, such as Jainism, take nonviolence so seriously that they clear their paths with brooms to avoid stepping on insects, and they wear masks to avoid inhaling insects.

Whereas Christianity views man as the master of the earth, superior to animals and plants, many Eastern traditions view man as custodian of the earth, connected to animals and plants.

MORALITY

There are moral implications to whether or not we have souls. For example, the Catholic church believes that abortion is wrong, that we become human when we receive souls, and that we receive souls at birth. However, until the 1800s, they believed that we receive souls at "quickening," around five months, when the fetus begins moving.

Other traditions believe that we become human when we are four months in the womb (Islam) or when we first take a breath (Judaism) or when we first receive names (some indigenous tribes). It is puzzling that conservative Christians have embraced this issue—which is clearly cultural—with such zeal, given the biblical ambivalence to the practice.

Many scholars believe that the test of the bitter waters in Numbers is the prescription of an abortifacient and they note that the penalty for killing a fetus in Exodus is less than the penalty for killing a human being. These passages suggest that the historical opposition to abortion had more to do with controlling the body of the woman than with protecting the life of the fetus.

Because Hindus focus on the absolute world more than the relative world and because they see divinity in everyone and everything, morality is relative. Is it wrong for the lion to kill the lamb? It seems right to the lion, but it seems wrong to the lamb.

If you believe, as many Hindus do, that God is in everyone and everything, and that we share our divinity with plants and animals, then there is not a bright line between man and animal, either—humans are made in God's image, as everything is. Killing is wrong, be it human or animal or plant. Many Eastern religions practice vegetarianism, so that they do not kill animals.

Recall that the mystics of all traditions encounter a reality that is whole, like the Eastern worldview, not a world that is broken or depraved or fallen, like the Western worldview.

SAINTS AND SAGES

In the West, many are more concerned with the relative world and the morality of individual behavior. To the extent that they profess the right beliefs or take the right actions, they hope to have eternal life. They likely revere saints, who refine the egoic self, as opposed to the True Self.

In the East, many are more concerned with the absolute world and the connection between everyone and everything. To the extent that they align themselves with the way of the Universe or the will of God, morality becomes less relevant, and they hope to do the right thing naturally. They likely revere sages, who realize the True Self, as opposed to the egoic self.

Absent egoic influences, we will act naturally, meaning that we behave in a manner that produces the least harm and/or the most help—that seeks harmony with the Oneness or the greater good—as opposed to following external prescriptions of right and wrong.

In business, we can do the right thing for ourselves or our bosses or our companies or our shareholders—who might all have different interests—or we can do the right thing for everyone—which is the natural thing, harmonious and unselfish.

It is easy to generate a false sense of security by relying on a moral code, but all moral codes deal in absolutes, such as those that decree that "thou shalt not kill." Shall we kill to advance a "just" war or to defend ourselves or to prevent further killing? What good is an absolute moral code if it only helps us to make the easy decisions?

Imagine that you are driving and an animal or a pedestrian darts in front of you. Perhaps you instinctively steer clear, without any time to be fearful or to develop a reaction. This is a natural response, not motivated by egoic concerns. Sometimes, we just need to get out of our own ways.

CHAPTER 13

HINDUISM

The Vedic tradition (commonly known as Hinduism) is one of the oldest traditions, deriving from the Vedas, the Upanishads, and the epic poems of ancient India.

PLURALISM

Hinduism describes a plethora of beliefs and practices. Hindus can be atheistic, monotheistic, or polytheistic; they can be dualistic or nondual; they can worship God in many forms. Hinduism can be seen as a polytheistic religion, but the many gods are thought to be manifestations of the One God or subordinate to the One God.

Within *Brahman* (the One) there is the Hindu trinity, consisting of Brahma (the creator), Vishnu (the sustainer), and Shiva (the destroyer). Some Hindus worship Ishvara, who can be seen as a personal god, and there are many deities with personal attributes.

There are sects that worship Vishnu and Shiva, and these two deities have feminine counterparts who are consorts, Lakshmi and Shakti. In Christianity, Wisdom is akin to the divine feminine in the Bible, and Mary is akin to the divine feminine in Catholicism.

Due to its diversity, Hinduism has a broader religious vocabulary than Christianity. Only people like philosopher Paul Tillich or mystic Meister Eckhart express Eastern concepts in Western terms. In Hinduism, the direct path to God is knowledge of the absolute aspect of God, called *jnana* or "wisdom," and the indirect path to God is love of the relative aspect of God, called *bhakti* or "devotion."

Sages like Ramakrishna believe that God is both personal and impersonal, that the essence of God is impersonal, and that knowledge of the impersonal is the direct path. Hindu sage Ramana Maharshi equated devotion and wisdom, writing, "To know God is to love God, therefore the paths of *jnana* and *bhakti* come to the same."

Nisargadatta Maharaj, a Hindu sage, described the essentiality of devotion and wisdom, writing, "Love says, 'I am Everything.' Wisdom says, 'I am Nothing.' Between the two, my life flows."

Author David Carse has an interesting perspective, that "There is a tradition that *jnana* is the higher path because the *bhakta* relies on a belief in someone or something to be devoted to, whereas the *jnani* knows there is neither. But true *bhakti* is pure devotion with no object; and the true *jnani* knows nothing."

Early in the spiritual journey, this statement might sound paradoxical, even nonsensical. As our understanding evolves, we realize that Carse sees impersonality and emptiness—no one to know (except everyone) and nothing to know (except everything). Here, impersonality does not mean lack of compassion or interest, but lack of partiality and separation.

AVATARS

In Hinduism, there can be an incarnation or manifestation of a deity, known as an avatar. Thus, Krishna and Ram are avatars of Vishnu, and other figures, such as Buddha and Jesus, are sometimes considered to be avatars.

> In the Christian tradition, the Father comes close to the absolute aspect of God.
>
> In the Christian tradition, the Holy Spirit comes close to the relative aspect of God.
>
> In the Christian tradition, Jesus comes close to the incarnation of an avatar.

There is a saying in the East that one should not confuse the moon with the finger pointing at the moon. Avatars point to God in the way that Jesus pointed to the Father (rather than to himself), because a being cannot embody the totality of the ground of being.

NONDUALITY

Shankara is an eighth century Hindu philosopher. Unlike Augustine and Anselm and Aquinas, who embellished Christian theology by addition, Shankara clarified Hindu theology by subtraction. Shankara reduced the many theologies of the Vedas, the Upanishads, and the epic poems to their common denominators.

Shankara outlined the philosophy of *Advaita Vedanta, Advaita* meaning nondual or "not two" and *Vedanta* meaning "the end of the Vedas" or "the end of knowledge." *Advaita Vedanta* is the foundation of many Hindu beliefs. Nonduality suggests that *Brahman* is a Oneness, where differentiation and separateness are illusions. He explains:

> There is the real Self, which is the eternal. But we do not realize our life as that of the real Self. Why do we not realize it? Because of two errors, or illusions, which make up the double heresy of separateness. The first error is the error of our separateness from the Eternal. The second error is the error of our separateness from each other.

Many years later, Rupert Spira, a spiritual teacher, writes much the same thing:

> The essential discovery of all the great spiritual traditions is the identity of Consciousness and Reality, the discovery that the fundamental nature of each one of us is identical with the fundamental nature of the Universe. This has been expressed as 'Atman equals Brahman,' 'I and my Father are one,' 'Nirvana equals Samsara,' 'Emptiness is Form,' 'I am That,' 'Consciousness is All,' 'There are not two things,' 'Sat Chit Ananda.'

Physicist Albert Einstein agreed, writing, "The separate self is an optical delusion in Consciousness."

Recall that the mystics of all traditions encounter nondual Oneness, like the Eastern worldview, not duality, like the Western worldview.

MAYA

In the East, the term *maya* means "illusion," the idea that things are not what they seem. Although there are radical *Advaitists* who believe that the material world does not exist, most believe that the material world is simply not as substantial as it appears. (If we believe that the material world does not exist, then we can become passive, and no one and nothing matters.)

The illusion is not the Universe itself, but the impression that we are separated from it. In the East, there is no good without evil or light without darkness, so when we attempt to divide one from another, we are distorting reality and separating the underlying Oneness.

Adyashanti and other spiritual teachers talk about an embodied or incarnated spirituality, in which one's practice is complete in bringing an awareness of the absolute world to the relative world. Many spiritual teachers, especially those who follow a *bhakti* or devotional path, emphasize compassion, as well as wisdom. Those with an embodied spirituality believe that the relative world matters, even if it is *maya*.

Recall that the mystics of all traditions encounter reality as a seamless field, like the Eastern worldview, not as a series of separate objects, like the Western worldview. Sometimes, people having mystical experiences perceive a sense of boundlessness, where they do not detect any boundary between their own bodies and the rest of the Universe.

ATMAN

The Self is a key idea in Hinduism. "The Self" (capital S) is the eternal Self, which is one with *Brahman*, and "the self" (small s) is the egoic self, which sees itself as separate. Some Hindus believe that *Atman* is *Brahman*, which is universal; others believe that *Atman* is particular, but not personal. Some Hindus believe that *Jivatman*, which is personal, is an aspect of *Atman*.

Some Hindus worship a personal god and believe that *Atman* (or *Jivatman*) is individual or personal too. In the West, many people worship a personal god and believe in personal souls. In fact, most traditions that believe in personal gods also believe in personal souls. This correspondence between how we see God and how we see ourselves leads some people to say that we create God in our own images, not vice versa.

Many Hindus, particularly those who believe that they have personal souls, believe that they reincarnate according to their *karma*. Others believe that they do not reincarnate; they simply merge into *Brahman*, like getting stirred into the cosmic soup. (Even those who believe in reincarnation believe that they merge into *Brahman* after they attain realization.)

Some people think that recollections of past lives constitute proof of reincarnation. If we recall a past life, how do we know that it is our personal life, rather than someone else's personal life or even everyone else's collective life?

Perhaps some people who died left larger impressions, and some people who live tune in to them, so that more people think they were Napoleon than think they were Napoleon's butler.

SELF-INQUIRY

In the East, Ramana Maharshi and others practice self-inquiry. "Who am I?" is such an inquiry. We soon realize that whatever we think we are (a conservative or a liberal, an extrovert or an introvert, a professional or a retiree), we are not eternally any of these things. All of these identities are ephemeral. Everything about our personality seems to be ephemeral, not eternal.

Thomas Merton, a Christian mystic, wrote, "Most of us live lives of self-impersonation." He explained:

> Who is this "I" that you imagine yourself to be? An easy
> and pragmatic branch of psychological thought will tell

you that if you can [say] your proper name, and declare that you are the bearer of that name, you know who you are…. But this is only a beginning…. For when a person appears to know his own name, it is still no guarantee that he is aware of the name as representing a real person. On the contrary, it may be the name of a fictitious character occupied in very active self-impersonation in the world of business, of politics, of scholarship or of religion.

To ask "Who am I?" is a simple, but profound, exercise. If you say "I am angry," ask yourself who is angry. Emotions such as anger are ephemeral, not eternal. These emotions arise from fear and regret, and we cannot locate the source of these thoughts.

When we peel away everything that we are not—I am not this, I am not that—all that is left is "I am," pure "is-ness," *Brahman* in Hinduism, God in Christianity, Yahweh in Judaism. In the East, the term "I am" for *Brahman* appears in the Upanishads, just as, in the West, the term "I am" for God appears in the Hebrew Bible.

CHAPTER 14

BUDDHISM AND TAOISM

Buddhism developed in response to Hinduism, which could be rigid and ritualistic. Hinduism began with the legitimate notion that everyone has their part to play, which soon devolved into the caste system, the damaging notion that everyone's part is predetermined. Throughout history, religions developed as reform movements. Christianity developed from Judaism, Islam developed from Christianity and Judaism. As old religions developed into new religions, new strands developed from the new religions. Thus, Christianity split into Eastern Orthodox, Catholicism, and Protestantism. Protestantism further split into Calvinism, Episcopalianism, and Methodism.

Buddhism split into Theravada, Mahayana, and Vajrayana strands. Each of these strands further split into other strands, such as Tibetan Buddhism and Zen Buddhism.

BUDDHA

Siddhartha Gautama was a spiritual seeker who found enlightenment under a bodhi tree, when he (now called the Buddha) attained liberation from *samsara,* the cycle of suffering. The Buddha is not a god, but a human being who realized Oneness. Buddhism is based on the notions of impermanence, suffering, and no-self.

On his deathbed, the Buddha instructed his followers not to follow any leaders, but to apply any teachings and to evaluate any instructions, even his own, with discernment.

Buddha developed a "middle way" between self-indulgence and self-mortification, based on The Four Noble Truths and The Noble Eightfold Path.

THE FOUR NOBLE TRUTHS

In Buddhism, there are Four Noble Truths: 1) Suffering is an innate characteristic of existence. 2) The cause of suffering is attachment, craving, and desire. 3) The cessation of suffering comes from ceasing attachment, craving, and desire. 4) The Noble Eightfold Path is the means to end suffering.

THE NOBLE EIGHTFOLD PATH

In Buddhism, the Noble Eightfold Path contains eight features:

1. Right view

2. Right intention

3. Right speech

4. Right action

5. Right livelihood

6. Right effort

7. Right mindfulness

8. Right meditation

The Noble Eightfold Path provides general guidelines, not specific prescriptions like the Ten Commandments. Buddhism is a practical framework for living a right life. There is no creed or hierarchy, and Buddhism is compatible with other traditions.

Alan Watts, an Episcopal priest and Zen practitioner, wrote:

The sections dealing with action are often misunderstood because they have a deceptive similarity to a "system of morals." Buddhism does not share the Western view that there is a moral law, enjoined by God or nature, which it is man's duty to obey. The Buddha's precepts of conduct... are voluntarily assumed rules of expediency, the intent of which is to remove the hindrances to clarity of awareness.

There is a false sense of security that arises from any absolute moral code. If we are not to kill and we are not to steal, may we kill to prevent further killing and may we steal to feed our families? Any absolute moral code, sacred or secular, does a terrific job of answering the easy questions and a terrible job of answering the difficult questions.

The Three Jewels of Buddhism are the three aspects of the awakened mind, namely the Buddha, the *dharma,* and the *sangha.* The Buddha is the teacher, the *dharma* is the teaching, and the *sangha* is the community.

The Buddha did not think that it was helpful to speculate about God or the afterlife, but many Buddhists have embraced the notion of rebirth. Some Buddhists believe that we are reborn, based on the *karma* of our past lives, until we reach *nirvana,* which is the end of suffering. After reaching *nirvana,* we merge into the Void.

Rebirth in Buddhism raises practical questions, like afterlife in Christianity or reincarnation in Hinduism. Because Buddhism holds that "self" is a construct, and rebirth suggests that some essence is reborn, what essence is reborn if it is not the "self?" If we go to heaven or hell or if we are reborn or reincarnated, what part of us transitions, if not our bodies and brains or our personalities and thoughts?

IMPERMANENCE

Buddha taught that everything is impermanent, so attachment produces suffering, primarily related to fear about the future and regret about the past. Here and now, the grass is growing, the sun is shining, and the wind is blowing, despite our fears and regrets.

Those who are new to Buddhism may think that "detachment" means indifference, but this is not a correct understanding. Buddhism is a compassionate tradition, and Buddhists care about all sentient beings, but love (according to the Buddha) is impersonal and unselfish, in that it does not involve clinging or grasping or possessing.

Author David Carse explains, "Even the concept 'compassion' can carry meanings of pity. But the Buddhist tradition has used the word to mean uninvolved, unattached openness to the best for all sentient forms without any thought of anything in return."

SUFFERING

Of course, we cannot eliminate the pains of death and illness and old age, but we can eliminate the suffering associated with them. Buddhists eliminate or reduce suffering by meditating, which involves clearing the mind, glimpsing the True Self, perceiving the Universe as it is, and recognizing the connection to the Universe.

Theravada Buddhism is oriented to monks who are striving for *nirvana* for themselves in a monastic setting. Mahayana Buddhism is oriented to people who are striving for *nirvana* as laypeople. In the Mahayana texts, those who delay *nirvana* for themselves, in order to assist others, are called *bodhisattvas*.

NO-SELF

In Buddhism, the concept of the self is unimportant. Buddhists seek "no-self," avoiding attachment to any concept of self and thereby reducing suffering. The notion of "emptiness" is related to the notion of no-self. Sometimes, Buddhists refer to emptiness as "the Void," which is how Christians describe the world before creation in the Bible.

It is helpful to interpret the Void to mean "without distinction or separation," rather than "without mass or energy." Emptiness refers to Oneness in Buddhism, just as fullness refers to Oneness in Hinduism.

Osho, an Indian mystic, explained:

Either you can be in existence or you can be in the self—both are not possible together. To be in the self means to be apart, to be separate. To be in the self means to become an island. To be in the self means to draw a boundary line around you. To be in the self means to draw a distinction between "this I am" and "this I am not."

Sometimes, those who are not familiar with the Eastern religions can be put off by terms such as "impersonal," so it can be helpful to think of "impersonal" to mean "impartial" or "undifferentiated." If we approach everyone in an impartial or undifferentiated manner, then we wipe the slate clean of any history with them, and we see them compassionately, here and now.

TAOISM

Taoism is an Eastern tradition that lives in harmony with the Tao or the Way. According to Kim-Kwong Chan, a Chinese religious scholar, Tao is "the One, which is natural, spontaneous, eternal, nameless, and indescribable. It is at once the beginning of all things and the way in which all things pursue their course."

In *Wen-tzu,* Lao Tzu distinguishes between our essential and seeming natures. In our essential natures (absolute) we are woven into the fabric of the Universe, and in our seeming (relative) natures, we can seem disconnected and divided.

Taoism emphasizes harmony with the Universe, and the concept of *wu wei* or "actionless action" is essential to Taoism. Actionless action means that no action is taken that is not in accord with the way of the Universe. Egoless action is actionless action.

Some Taoist texts present water as a metaphor for the highest virtues. Water can be strong, but it can also be supportive. Water seeks the lowest point and takes the natural course. Water forms deep pools, and water reflects its surroundings when it is still and undisturbed. Water accommodates obstacles, and water is available to all, without discrimination.

The *Tao Te Ching* describes the ineffability of Tao:

> The Tao that can be told is not the eternal Tao;
> The name that can be named is not the eternal name.
> The nameless is the beginning of heaven and earth;
> The named is the mother of ten thousand things.

"The name that cannot be named" is reminiscent of the apophatic or negative theology of Hinduism ("Not this, not that"). Also, "the Tao" and "the ten thousand things" are reminiscent of the absolute and the relative of Buddhism and Hinduism.

Taoism uses the yin and yang symbol to say that the One consists of polarities: the yin is cold, dark, feminine, and passive; the yang is the hot, light, masculine, and active. Polar opposites are united in perfect harmony in the circle of yin and yang.

The yin and the yang are a unified whole. Ken Wilber, a Buddhist philosopher, writes that yin and the yang do not exist separately, as buying and selling do not exist separately.

In the *Heart Sutra*, a seminal text in the Mahayana tradition, the Buddhists have a similar understanding, saying, "Form is emptiness, emptiness is not different from form, neither is form different from emptiness, indeed, emptiness is form." Emptiness and form cannot exist separately, just as the yin and the yang cannot exist separately.

Ramakrishna, a Hindu mystic and sage, speaks of the absolute and the relative in similar terms, saying that "Both the absolute and the relative belong to one and the same Reality."

When we see how compatible the Eastern worldview is with Oneness, then we also see how incompatible the Western worldview is with Oneness. Beginning in Genesis, everything is separated—light and dark, earth and water, plants and animals, animals and man. Later, in the church, people are separated—Christians and non-Christians, clergy and laity, men and women, straight and LGBTQ people.

EAST AND WEST

The Eastern and the Western worldviews are very different, and (in some ways) they cannot both be true. For instance, either the Universe was created or it is eternal. Either we have free will, selves, and souls, or we do not. Either we are extinguished, reborn or reincarnated, sent to heaven or hell, or stirred into the cosmic soup.

Once one embraces nondual Eastern notions, then dualistic Western notions—such as good and evil or heaven and hell—become problematic. How can God be three persons? How can God be separate from creation? How can God and humans be separated by original sin? How can humans be separated from everyone and everything in the Universe?

Would the personal god of Western theology really devise an 80-year test for each one of us to determine our eternal destiny? Would the impersonal Universe of Eastern theology really devise an 80-year test for each one of us to determine our next life?

We have explored how the mystics of all traditions and how the Eastern religions, such as Buddhism, Hinduism, and Taoism, understand the metaphysical Universe. Does any of this correspond to our modern understanding of the physical universe? Enter the scientists.

Sannyasa
(The Renunciant)

During the fourth stage of life, a person renounces all desires, duties, fears, hopes, and responsibilities, in order to live a life that is totally devoted to God.

—

After all of my reading, I was looking for something more experiential than intellectual, which led me to the Camino de Crestone, an inter-spiritual pilgrimage in Crestone, Colorado.

Crestone, a small town at the base of the Sangre de Cristo Mountains in southern Colorado, is home to numerous spiritual centers, including several Buddhist centers, a Carmelite hermitage (now closed), a Hindu ashram, and a Shinto healing center.

The Camino de Crestone is a weeklong walk among the centers, in which a small group of pilgrims engage in discussions, participate in ceremonies, and receive teachings.

When we returned home after a week of exercise, fresh air, good food, great company, meaningful experiences, and stimulating conversations, someone asked how it felt to be back in the real world "That was the real world," we said. "This isn't real. It's just bills and bosses and budgets, technology and tension and traffic."

In Crestone, it is common to meet people who associate with a few traditions—a person might be a member of the ashram and the hermitage and the Sufi circle. There is a common appreciation for the perennial philosophy, the notion that all spiritual traditions spring from the same source.

Crestone is a special place, and we have returned several times since our first visit. Many of those experiences clarified my thinking, and much of this book was written there. Most of the following experiences took place in Crestone over the last few years.

THE WAY OF NATURE

John P. Milton is an ecologist, meditation master, and spiritual teacher who developed a program called The Way of Nature, and an intensive journey called Sacred Passage, which teaches The Way of Nature through a twelve-day retreat.

When I met John Milton, I was struck by his presence. John is comfortable in his own skin, and his actions and words are deliberate, yet natural. He has an equanimity that I have seen in few other people. Although it is uncommon to meet people like this, I met several in Crestone.

Milton conducts retreats on land that is known for its *chi* or primordial energy. (*Chi* or *qi* in the Taoist tradition is similar to *prana* in the Vedic tradition and *ruah* in the Jewish tradition.) Milton believes that the land is sacred and that the rocks conduct *chi*.

When our guide said that the Spirit is present in the rocks, I asked if the Spirit is present everywhere or if the Spirit is unique to each rock, and she answered "Yes, and yes."

THE SINGING STONE

Chris Long is a medicine man of Cherokee and Choctaw descent who holds sweat lodge ceremonies. He is a spiritual person, who has experienced, read, and reflected a lot. The ceremonies are held in a small hut that is heated by hot stones to over 100 degrees.

Blankets cover the door, and water is poured over hot stones, while the medicine man chants and drums in the darkened sweat lodge.

During the ceremony, one of the women in our group had a vision of a white wolf. To her, the wolf symbolized her lone nature, and the color suggested her return to purity. "Everything is energy," Chris said, "and we all perceive the energy differently." This makes sense to me.

The typical mystical experience is impersonal, but to the extent that we personalize it (or that we see the absolute mystery in a relative manner), we see what we expect to see. In a church, we might see Jesus, and in a hot sweat lodge, we might see a wolf. We might see Spirit everywhere, or we might see Spirit in a rock.

HAIDAKHANDI UNIVERSAL ASHRAM

The Haidakhandi Universal Ashram was created to preserve the teachings of Haidakhan Baba or Babaji. Babaji was a young man in India between 1970 and 1984, and he was believed to be an avatar of Shiva, who has taken human form many times.

I participated in several *aartis* and fire ceremonies at the ashram, chanting to Babaji, to the Divine Mother, and to Shiva. While many at the ashram believe that Babaji was a divine incarnation, the rest of us could chant to Babaji whether we believed that or not, and we could chant to Shiva to worship our own God or gods. In the Hindu tradition, everything is *Brahman*, and *Brahman* has many manifestations.

SRI AUROBINDO LEARNING CENTER

The Sri Aurobindo Learning Center was established to preserve the teachings of Aurobindo, a twentieth century Indian philosopher who joined the movement for independence from British rule, and became a spiritual teacher after independence.

He was an integral philosopher who sought an understanding of the Universe, like Ken Wilber in the Buddhist tradition or Teilhard de Chardin in the Christian tradition. When you talk to people at the Aurobindo Center, you realize that Eastern philosophers know much more about our Western worldview than we know about theirs. (Sometimes it seems that they know even more about the Western worldview than we do.)

SHUMEI INTERNATIONAL INSTITUTE

Shumei International Institute is associated with the Japanese Shinto tradition, and Shumei focuses on artistic expression, spiritual practices, and sustainable agriculture.

Shumei hosts Taiko drumming concerts, and this "thunder drumming" can prompt altered states and the cessation of thought, like chanting in the Vedic tradition, repetitive prayer in the Christian tradition, and "whirling" in the Muslim tradition.

Also, Shumei hosts *jyorei* sessions, which are spiritual energy healing ceremonies that involve phonetic chanting and intense focusing of spiritual light to dispel darkness. The idea that energy can be focused and used to heal makes sense to me, although I cannot explain it.

GOLDEN LIGHT SUFI CIRCLE

The Golden Light Sufi Circle is a group of Sufi Muslims. Sufis are the mystics of Islam, known for their ecstatic dancing or "whirling." Rumi was a well-known Sufi poet, and Ibn Arabi was a well-known Sufi philosopher. Both are regarded as mystics.

When we took part in a *dhikr*, we chanted to Allah, as we had chanted to Shiva, and this, too, felt like worshiping the One. We also whirled, and the chanting and the whirling produced altered states, unlike anything that I ever found in church.

CHINESE ZEN TEA CEREMONY

William Howell, the founder of the Camino de Crestone, invited us to attend tea ceremonies in the Chinese Zen tradition, with a meditation centered around the flavors, sights, smells, sounds, and textures of the tea.

The tea is grown and harvested by Buddhist monks and nuns in remote areas of China. The trees are hundreds of years old, the tea is believed to contain *chi* or energy, and it is cultivated with mindfulness.

The tea serves to focus the meditation, and although meditation does not usually come easily for me, the tea helped me to focus. When meditation is communal, rather than individual, there is a sense of energy and intimacy. The practice develops a sense of connectedness, unlike anything that I ever found in church.

TEYUNA MAMOS

During one trip to Crestone, we spent a few days with the *mamos* or spiritual leaders of the Teyuna tribe, an indigenous tribe in the coastal highlands of Colombia, learning about their healing abilities, meditative practices, and wisdom traditions.

Teyuna means "thinker of clear thoughts," and the tribe was featured in an insightful documentary called *The Heart of the World,* available on YouTube. The *mamos* are selected at birth, and they spend the first nine years of their lives in caves, learning their peoples' wisdom.

The Teyuna consider themselves to be elder brothers to the rest of the world, and they feel responsible to alert their younger brothers (us) to the perils of deforestation and other environmental degradation.

After the retreat, the Teyuna were asked to name the biggest challenge to their way of life, and (instead of climate change, global pandemics, or nuclear wars) they said "Evangelization."

This is a common view among indigenous people, who have lost their cultures to Christian evangelists and Western "progress." In some traditions, if you help someone who does not want to be helped, you commit an act of violence (regardless of your intention.)

NADA HERMITAGE

The Nada Hermitage was run by the Carmelites, a Roman Catholic religious order focused on contemplation. John of the Cross and Teresa of Avila, prominent Spanish mystics in the 1500s, were Carmelites.

A candid conversation with a Carmelite priest revealed that many clergy and laity are not comfortable with some church doctrine and that we will likely not see much reform in our lifetimes.

We agreed that Christianity (particularly Catholicism) emphasizes separation, whereas most other traditions emphasize oneness; and that Christianity (particularly Catholicism) does not address suffering as well as most other traditions. In Christianity, suffering is embraced, almost wel-comed. "Jesus suffered" or "Jesus joins us in our suffering" or "Suffering has a purpose" or "Suffering will be rewarded in the hereafter."

—

After making several pilgrimages to Crestone, I began to wonder whether there might be opportunities for more experiential and mystical spiri-tualities closer to home, so I was delighted to find that there is a well-known Zen teacher only 20 miles from where we live.

MARIA KANNON ZEN CENTER

Ruben Habito is a former Jesuit priest who is now a professor of religion at Southern Methodist University (SMU) and a Zen teacher at the Maria Kannon Zen Center (MKZC). He wrote several books that integrate Bud-dhist and Christian beliefs and practices.

Zen is a practice, not a belief system. Some aspects of Zen practice fit with Christian beliefs, and some aspects of Christian beliefs fit with Zen practice. Like many practice-based traditions, Zen highlights the role of the teacher, who provides guidance on the spiritual journey.

Before I became a student at the Zen Center, my knowledge of Zen was limited, and it seemed too enigmatic and too spartan for me. Now that I am more comfortable with paradox and less comfortable with doc-trine, Zen practice is the best—perhaps the only—path for me. Looking back, I see that I wrote a Zen book (this one) without meaning to do so.

CHAPTER 15

THE SCIENTISTS

Many scholars interpret the Bible stories allegorically, metaphorically, or mythically. Theologian John Dominic Crossan writes, "My point is not that those ancient people told literal stories and we are now smart enough to take them symbolically, but that they told them symbolically and we are now dumb enough to take them literally."

As scientists learn more about the biology, chemistry, and physics of the universe, our new understandings cast doubt on literal interpretations of the Bible.

EVOLUTION

Many Christians used to believe that the Earth is 6,000 years old, but science tells us that the universe is 14 billion years old and the Earth is 4 billion years old.

Many Christians used to believe that God created the plants, animals, and human beings in seven days, but science tells us that humans evolved over 3.5 billion years.

Many Christians used to believe that the Earth was once a Garden of Eden, but science tells us that there was no original perfection.

Many Christians used to believe that Adam lived 6,000 years ago, but science tells us that human beings have lived on the earth for over 200,000 years.

Many Christians used to believe that all human beings descended from one man, Adam, and one woman, Eve, who were exiled from the Garden of Eden for eating an apple, but science tells us that all humans descended from one man (called "Y-chromosome Adam," who lived approximately 210,000 years ago) and one woman (called "Mitochondrial Eve," who lived approximately 180,000 years ago).

Adam and Eve likely did not bite the same apple, and Eve was likely not around to urge Adam to take the bite. This story is almost certainly a myth. Could a mythical man and a mythical woman commit an actual sin by biting a mythical apple?

Of course, myths can contain truth, even if they are not based on history, in the same way that fictional accounts can contain truth, even if they are not based on history. Still, we should be clear about when we are speaking mythically, rather than literally.

If the universe evolved messily and randomly, then it was not perfect at the start, and there was no fall from perfection to ordinariness. If it was not perfect at the start, then how could it be perfect at the end? If the Earth will eventually be restored, to what state will it revert?

Even more troubling, if there was no original sin, then there was no need for Jesus to die to redeem our sins. If we evolved slowly, rather than suddenly, then did our souls—if we have souls—evolve?

Science tells us that there were once several types of human beings living at the same time and that human beings could eventually evolve into more advanced beings. Singer Tom Waits says that "We are all just monkeys with money and guns."

Those who think that we are the culmination of creation or that we were singularly created in God's image should take a longer view—only 50,000 years ago, homo sapiens were climbing trees for food, communicating in grunts, and copulating with Neanderthals.

GEOCENTRICITY

Many Christians used to believe that Earth is the center of the universe, that the universe was created only for us, that there was no possibility of life elsewhere, and that heaven was in the sky and hell was underground.

Science tells us that there could be 40 billion habitable planets in the galaxy, that species may be more advanced than ours, and that there is no heaven above or hell below. If there is intelligent life on other planets, that raises the question of whether Jesus is the savior of the Earth or the savior of the universe.

Thomas Paine was a deist author in the eighteenth century who rejected divine providence (God's involvement in human affairs) and supernaturalism. In *Common Sense*, Paine irreverently wondered:

> From whence, then, could arise the solitary and strange conceit that the Almighty, who had millions of worlds equally dependent on his protection, should quit the care of all the rest, and come to die in our world, because, they say, one man and one woman had eaten an apple? And, on the other hand, are we to suppose that every world in the boundless creation had an Eve, an apple, a serpent, and a redeemer? In this case, the person who is irreverently called the Son of God, and sometimes God himself, would have nothing else to do than to travel from world to world, in an endless succession of deaths, with scarcely a momentary interval of life.

Is there intelligent life in the universe? The conditions for life are very specific, and there would have to be many attempts over a long time, if any were to succeed. However, eternity is a long time, and infinity is a long way. Given enough space and time, life might randomly appear in many different places at many different times.

Some say that the Universe is continuously learning, as possibilities evolve into realities, and that memories of past realities might impact future realities.

It is unlikely that we are the only intelligent life in the universe. Would God spend 14 billion years creating a universe just for us, even if we could never see it all, and even if we could destroy ourselves with climate change, global pandemics, or nuclear wars?

GOD OF THE GAPS

Many Christians used to believe that souls controlled our bodies, but science tells us that virtually all of our experience is attributable to biology, chemistry, and physics.

Many Christians used to believe in a "God of the gaps" who was likely responsible for any events that we could not explain otherwise. As science explains more events, there are fewer events that we cannot explain, thus fewer gaps for God to fill, except for three big questions that will likely never be resolved:

We do not know what started the Big Bang—or whether there actually was one—and scientists have not determined whether it required an external cause.

We do not know how life on earth began—and we may never know—and scientists have not determined whether it required an external cause.

We do not know how we acquired sentience—and we may never know—but it would be easier to determine that than to determine what started the Big Bang or how life began.

Imagine that the Big Bang occurred naturally as part of the continuous creation and destruction of the Universe. In some ways, that is an even more amazing story.

Imagine that life began when a lightning strike activated a simple organism in a nutrient-rich sea. In some ways, that is an even more amazing story.

Imagine that sentience developed naturally, as increasingly complex organs evolved. In some ways, that is an even more amazing story.

If the beginning of the Universe, the beginning of life, and the emergence of sentience all occurred naturally—rather than supernaturally, through the action or design of a Creator—would the amazing complexity and diversity and interconnectivity of the Universe be any less astounding? Would we be any less grateful for an amazing world of natural, rather than supernatural, origin?

INTERCONNECTEDNESS

Scientists say that biology is derived from chemistry, which is derived from physics, which is derived from mathematics. It seems that everything is connected, and photos of the Earth from space pointedly remind us that we share this planet. Climate change, global pandemics, and nuclear wars reveal our interconnectedness.

In *The Hidden Life of Trees*, forester Peter Wohlleben describes how plants and animals in the forest depend on each other. He writes, "When you know that trees experience pain and have memories and that tree parents live together with their children, then you can no longer just chop them down and disrupt their lives with large machines...." He continues:

> Why are trees such social beings? Why do they share food with their own species and sometimes even go so far as to nourish their competitors? The reasons are the same as for human communities: there are advantages to working together. A tree is not a forest. On its own, a tree cannot establish a consistent local climate. It is at the mercy of wind and weather. But together, many trees create an ecosystem that moderates extremes of heat and cold, stores a great deal of water, and generates a great deal of humidity. And in this protected environment, trees can live to be very old.

Within organisms, science tells us that cells exchange information with their environments not through the nuclei of the cells, but through the membrane of the cells. Cells coordinate to allow the organs to function, and organs coordinate to allow the organism itself to function.

Biologist Bruce Lipton explains, "You may consider yourself an individual, but as a cell biologist, I can tell you that you are in truth a cooperative community of approximately 50 trillion single-celled citizens."

Science tells us that the input from our senses is processed in our brains, so we experience life in our heads, not in our eyes or ears or hands. Our brains are networks, and there is no controller. Clearly, our brains handle many processes, like beating our hearts, digesting our food, and working our lungs, without any direction from our selves or our souls.

We have memories, but they are not stored in particular places in our brains, and they are not recorded precisely. Our memories of the past are no more precise than our imaginings about the future.

HUMANITY

Science tells us that organisms communicate with each other. For example, consider the almost seamless communication in an ant nest or a beehive. In humans, the Global Consciousness Project at Princeton found disruptions in random number generators that coincide with disruptive events, such as the 9/11 attack.

That is, generators that have been consistently generating random numbers begin producing numbers in non-random sequence during periods of societal stress.

The Maharishi Effect, named for Maharishi Mahesh Yogi, found correlations between meditations by large groups and notable reductions in the incidence of crime. Of course, correlation does not necessarily suggest causation, and these experiments are difficult to control or replicate, but the findings are thought-provoking.

Although scientists have not been able to definitively prove the efficacy of prayer, there is anecdotal evidence that intention (for non-theists) or prayer (for theists) can influence outcomes, by altering the way of the Universe or the will of God, respectively.

If we are part of a connected field, and if consciousness impacts matter, and if we communicate in subtle ways, then it stands to reason that intention or prayer might have efficacy.

CHAPTER 16

THE QUANTUM PHYSICISTS

Science continues to evolve, particularly in the emerging field of quantum physics. Physicist Niels Bohr famously said, "Anyone who is not shocked by quantum theory has not understood it." Biologist J.B.S. Haldane famously agreed, "The Universe is not only queerer than we suppose, but queerer than we can suppose."

At the same time that science is challenging fundamental aspects of the Western worldview, science is confirming fundamental aspects of the Eastern worldview. Fritjof Capra wrote an influential book called *The Tao of Physics,* describing the parallels between Eastern mysticism and modern physics, especially quantum physics:

> A consistent view of the world is beginning to emerge from modern physics which is harmonious with ancient Eastern wisdom.... Quantum theory thus reveals a basic oneness of the Universe. It shows that we cannot decompose the world into independently existing smallest units. As we penetrate into matter, nature does not show us any isolated "basic building blocks," but rather appears as a complicated web of relations between the various parts of the whole.... Mystics understand the roots of the Tao but not its branches; scientists understand its branches but not its roots. Science does not need mysticism and mysticism does not need science; but man needs both.

RELIGION AND SCIENCE

The Eastern worldview is less dogmatic and more paradoxical—thus more robust—and the vocabulary of the Eastern religions is broader and deeper, addressing concepts such as absolute or relative and destiny or free will and emptiness or fullness.

These are concepts that are not addressed fully (if at all) in the Western religions, so there are a lot of significant conversations with some followers of Eastern religions in which most followers of Western religions do not fully participate.

As I discuss ideas in quantum physics, I will relate them to ideas in Hinduism, since this tradition has the richest vocabulary and best reflects the perennial philosophy.

Eastern religions and quantum physics do not "prove" or "validate" each other, but the consistency between the Oneness that Eastern religions see in the metaphysical world and the oneness that quantum physicists see in the physical world is striking.

THE FIELD

In Newtonian physics, things are discrete objects, interacting like billiard balls. Systems are atomistic or reductionist; the whole is the sum of the parts. In quantum physics, things are linked in an interconnected field, a oneness. Systems are holistic or relational; the whole is in the parts and the parts are in the whole.

We are relearning that our world is connected, as we grapple with climate change, global pandemics, and nuclear wars. In *The Luminous Web*, Barbara Brown Taylor, an Episcopal priest, describes God in terms of the new physics:

> God is all over the place. God is up there, down here, inside my skin and out. God is the web, the energy, the space, the light—not captured in them, as if those concepts were more real than what unites them—but revealed in that singular, vast net of relationships that animates everything that is.

Almost 2,000 years ago, Emperor Marcus Aurelius, a Stoic philosopher, wrote, "Everything is connected, and the web is holy."

THE NEW PHYSICS

Experiments have shown that observers influence outcomes and that observers are not disconnected from what they observe. At one level, observers can alter objects in the process of observing them, such as when the light beams that are aimed at objects move the objects.

At another level, observers can see a photon as either a particle or a wave, depending on whether the observer is measuring particle properties or wave properties. The notion that observers influence outcomes supports the efficacy of intention or prayer.

Gary Zukav, a spiritual teacher, talks about the new physics:

> May the universe in some strange sense be "brought into being" by the participation of those who participate?... The vital act is the act of participation. "Participator" is the incontrovertible new concept given by quantum mechanics. It strikes down the term "observer" of classical theory, the man who stands safely behind the glass wall and watches what goes on without taking part.

We do not experience the world directly; we experience the world indirectly, through senses. Whereas the Western worldview, from Descartes, divides the world into matter and mind (so-called "substance dualism"), the Eastern worldview combines mind and matter in nonduality, not dualism. All is *Brahman*.

The Hindus might say that everyone is related, and everything is connected. Separation is an illusion. Because we are in the world and the world is in us, our viewpoint is subjective.

—

The field contains both energy and matter, but energy and matter are interchangeable, as Einstein documented in his famous equation,

$E = mc^2$. As physicists explore atoms, they realize that they are composed of subatomic particles and that they are mostly empty space, not matter. Solid objects are not really "solid."

According to physicist Richard Feynman, there is enough energy in a cubic meter of space to boil all of our oceans. Emptiness is not really "empty" either.

The Hindus might say that the relative world (*maya*) is not as substantial as it appears. Also, change is constant, and everything from the cells in our body to the galaxies in our Universe are constantly changing form and recycling between energy and matter. As the Buddhists say, "Form is emptiness, and emptiness is form."

———

Now, quantum physics gets even stranger. Experiments have shown that (at the atomic level) energy and matter exhibit the qualities of both waves and particles. The waves that we associate with matter are probability waves, so that when we view an electron as a wave, then we must describe its location as a probability function of the electron's possible locations.

The Hindus might say that this paradox is akin to absolute (wave) and relative (particle) realities. If matter (in our relative reality) is probabilistic, then much of life (in our relative reality) is probabilistic, too. Our lives are not entirely deterministic, and they are not entirely random either.

———

In the East, it is common to say that we are like waves (that are ephemeral) in an ocean (that is eternal) and that the ocean is always contained in the wave and vice versa. Some say that when we die we merge into the Universe, like waves merge into the ocean, and although waves constantly reappear, the "same" waves do not reappear.

If we are "stirred into the cosmic soup," it seems unlikely that we would retain any individuality or personhood. After all, we probably do not take our bodies and brains or our personalities and thoughts with us when we die.

SPACE/TIME

Experiments have shown that scientists can measure a particle's location or its momentum, but not both, and that space and time are really a space/time continuum.

Gary Zukav, a spiritual writer, hypothesizes:

> If we could view our reality in a four-dimensional way, we would see everything that now seems to unfold before us with the passing of time, already exists in toto, painted, as it were, on the fabric of space-time. We would see all, the past, the present, and the future with one glance. Of course, this is only a mathematical proposition (isn't it?).

Experiments have also shown that space, time, and space/time are relative, meaning that space and time are measured differently in different places and speeds, so that space and time appear differently to observers in different places.

The Hindus might say that physical relativity is analogous to moral relativity, that both depend on perspective. In the absolute world, there is only Oneness, so space and time might be meaningless to a scientist, and morality might be meaningless to a mystic. However, in the relative world, which we experience every day, space and time are meaningful to a scientist, and morality is meaningful to a mystic.

———

Quantum physics gets stranger, still. Some outcomes can be predicted with accuracy and some outcomes are probability functions until they are observed. In fact, the quantum world is probabilistic, not deterministic or random.

Schrödinger's Cat is a thought experiment where a cat is in a box, and there is an equal probability that the cat is alive or dead—which paradoxically means that it is both—until the probability function collapses, and the cat's fate is determined.

The Hindus might say that causal outcomes derive from *karma* and that random outcomes derive from chance.

ENTANGLEMENT

In the subatomic realm, particles can become "quantum entangled," which means that when two particles are related—and perhaps all particles are related—then one entangled particle can influence another entangled particle, no matter their distance, and the impact is instantaneous, at least as fast as the speed of light. Albert Einstein called this phenomenon "spooky action at a distance."

The Hindus might say that we are not as individual or separate as we think we are, if particles and groups of particles are entangled with other particles and groups of particles. (In fact, because the Big Bang likely began as a singularity, we may all be entangled.)

Outside of theological speculation, would we have any evidence to suggest that we have selves, souls, or free will? Well, it certainly seems so—but then, it seems like the sun revolves around the earth and like the earth is standing still; but then, it seems like this table is solid and like those particles are not entangled.

Imagine that God is the architecture, rather than the architect, of the Universe. Imagine that this God is manifest as consciousness in the metaphysical world and as energy in the physical world. In this Web, where everyone and everything is connected, notions such as self, soul, and free will are simply constructs, unnecessary separations.

CHAPTER 17

Consciousness

Philosopher David Chalmers writes, "Consciousness poses the most baffling problems in the science of mind. There is nothing that we know more intimately than conscious experience, but there is nothing that is harder to explain."

Author Annaka Harris offers one possible explanation:

> Is it possible that alongside the conscious experience of "me," there is a much dimmer experience of each individual neuron or of different collections of neurons and cells in my body and beyond? Could the universe literally be teeming with consciousness flickering in and out, overlapping, combining, separating, flowing, in ways we can't quite imagine—depending on the laws of physics in a way we don't yet understand?

The mystics describe a state of cosmic consciousness or unity consciousness, in which we are able to transcend our egoic selves and to attain a sense that everyone is related, and everything is connected. This cosmic consciousness is sometimes known as "Buddha nature" in Buddhism or "Christ consciousness" in Christianity.

SOULS

Some Christians believe that our souls will survive our deaths, but souls are philosophical, rather than religious, concepts. Aristotle said that souls are the life forces that animate all beings:

- The nutritive soul governed growth in plants, animals, and humans.

- The sensitive soul governed sensation in animals and humans.

- The rational soul governed thought in humans.

As scientists have now attributed growth and sensation to biology, chemistry, and physics, the first two notions of soul have collapsed, and only the third notion remains.

Further, evolution raises the question of whether animals have souls. If animals and humans were created at the same time, then animals might not have souls, but if animals evolved into humans over time, then how and when did souls evolve?

Does everyone have a soul? In the same way that some human beings have extra or missing fingers and toes, could some human beings have extra or missing souls? How would we know if our souls were damaged, since there is no evidence that we even have souls?

Some theologians claim that souls are immortal, without knowing what a soul is or where it resides. Scientists have not found any evidence of an immortal soul, separate from a mortal body, and they attribute sentience to consciousness, not to souls.

Julien Musolino, a psychologist who wrote *The Soul Fallacy*, writes:

> Notice that the conclusion, if we want to be intellectually honest, should not be that there is no soul, but rather, that there are no good reasons to believe that we have souls, and that there are very good reasons to believe that we do not have souls.... In the end, the soul, like the emperor's new clothes, has exactly the properties that it should have if it didn't exist.

Most scientists are only interested in the soul to the extent that there is evidence of its presence or proof of its actions—so there is not a science of the soul, per se. In fact, what is the practical relevance of the soul, if neither the soul nor its actions are visible?

FREE WILL

The concept of individuality or personhood or self is key to the Western worldview, as is the related concept of free will. Most of us believe that we have free will, until we realize that our thoughts come to us. We do not decide to think our thoughts, any more than we decide to breathe our air or to digest our food.

Scientists tell us that 95 percent of our thoughts come from our subconscious minds, and that most of the thoughts that come from our conscious minds derive from either nature or nurture. We are products of conditioning, slaves to habits and instincts.

As we learned earlier, the physicists tell us that we are entangled with everything, so that even if we think we are acting independently, we might be responding to someone or something with which we are entangled, across the room or across the universe.

Scientists have studied how much time passes between when we decide to do something and when we actually do it. Often, we "decide" to do something up to ten seconds AFTER we do it, which means that our brains are not deciding what to do; they are reporting what we have done. Do we really have free will? No. At least, we do not have as much free will as we think we have.

Philosopher Arthur Schopenhauer hit the nail on the head, as usual, when he wrote, "A man can surely do what he wills to do, but he cannot determine what he wills."

Physicist Stanley Sobottka discusses duality and free will, writing, "Notice that the concept of free will can only arise if there is an agent that is separate from its surrounding circumstances. This separation is the essence of duality. Without duality, there is neither the agent nor that which is acted upon, so free will has no meaning."

Salvadore Poe, a spiritual teacher, warns of the pitfalls of free will, saying, "This is why the world is such a mess, because everybody thinks they're the doer with free will. Then everyone blames everyone else because they think they're the doer with free will."

If we do not have free will, or at least if we do not have as much free will as we think we have, are we simply floating "gently down the stream," as the song says?

Perhaps we can adjust course, as if we are paddling around a rapid or pushing off from a big rock.

Perhaps we can cultivate mindfulness and eliminate attachments, so that we can respond to the will of God (from a theistic perspective) or to the way of the Universe (from a nontheistic perspective).

Perhaps we can develop good influences and establish good habits, so that through the forces of nature and nurture and through the influences of our entanglements and our subconscious minds, we can best respond to the will of God or to the way of the Universe.

The notion that we do not independently and intentionally control our actions or our thoughts has momentous theological implications. If we do not control our actions or our thoughts, then would a just and merciful God punish or reward our behavior?

This notion also has momentous practical implications in the here and now. If we do not control our actions or our thoughts, then should our societal response to addictions or crimes or poverty be more therapeutic than punitive?

SELF-ACTUALIZATION

In 1943, psychologist Abraham Maslow proposed a hierarchy of needs, suggesting the following:

- human beings need to satisfy their physiological needs (clothing, food, shelter)

- before they can satisfy their safety needs (emotional, financial, health)

- before they can satisfy their social needs (family, friends, intimacy)

- before they can satisfy their self-esteem needs (freedom, independence, mastery)

- before they can reach self-actualization, the realization of one's full potential.

After he died, Maslow's book *The Farther Reaches of Human Nature* was released, in which Maslow suggested that self-actualization is not the final step in development. Rather, once we are self-actualized, we can transcend our "narrative selves," devoting ourselves to something bigger than ourselves, such as altruism or service or spirituality.

Maslow also distinguishes between the "transcenders" and "non-transcending self-actualizers" (whom he calls "merely healthy people") and he observes that transcenders are typically more holistic, more intimate, more loving, and more natural.

Philosopher Ken Wilber similarly describes an evolution of consciousness from "me" to "us" to "all of us," or from egocentric to ethno-centric to world-centric. In most theories of human development, the pinnacle is a perspective that embraces oneness.

In all traditions, we die to the self. In meditation, we focus on thoughts to detach from them. In Buddhism, we abandon the boat after we cross the river, and we kill the Buddha if we ever meet him. (Of course, this is a euphemism. We never meet the Buddha, only our concepts of the Buddha.)

Alan Watts, an Episcopal priest and Zen practitioner, observed that as Zen became popular, "The Zen community became less an association of mature men with spiritual interests, and more of an ecclesiastical boarding school for adolescent boys." Zen incorporated discipline to initially develop a sense of self, so that (with maturity) practitioners could eventually detach from this sense of self.

In *Man's Search for Meaning,* psychiatrist Viktor Frankl wrote:

> [B]eing human always points, and is directed, to something or someone, other than oneself—be it a meaning to fulfill or another human being to encounter. The more one forgets himself—by giving himself to a cause to serve or another person to love—the more human he is and the more he actualizes himself.

HOLINESS OR WHOLENESS

Sometimes, Christians will say that they want to be great or perfect or sinless (or that they cannot be any of those things, so they only hope that their imperfect, sinful selves will receive God's grace). This is self-actualization, but it is not transcendence.

"Congratulations," we might say. "I hope that you find greatness or perfection or sinlessness, but when you perfect your self, destroy your self; when you actualize your self, transcend your self." When we transcend ourselves, we realize our wholeness.

SPIRITUAL EVOLUTION

Theologian James Fowler listed the stages of faith development:

Stage 0—"Primal or Undifferentiated" faith (birth to two years) displays a concern with safety

Stage 1—"Intuitive-Projective" faith (three to seven years) displays a fluidity of thought

Stage 2—"Mythic-Literal" faith (school-age children) displays a literalization of metaphors

Stage 3—"Synthetic-Conventional" faith (adolescence) displays a conformity to authority

Stage 4—"Individuative-Reflective" faith (young adult) displays a questioning of beliefs

Stage 5—"Conjunctive" faith (midlife) displays an acceptance of ambiguity and paradox

Stage 6—"Universalizing" faith displays a universal concern for justice and mercy

Not everyone progresses through each of these stages. In fact, some traditions emphasize authority structures or literal interpretations, which can impede development. When we have a universalizing faith, we reach the highest level of development.

In *How to Change Your Mind,* author Michael Pollan writes, "The usual antonym for the word 'spiritual' is 'material.' Now, I'm inclined to think a much better and certainly more useful antonym for 'spiritual' might be 'egotistical.'" He continues:

> When the ego dissolves, so does a bounded conception not only of our self but of our self-interest. What emerges in its place is invariably a broader, more openhearted and altruistic—that is, more spiritual—idea of what matters in life. One in which a new sense of connection, of love, however defined, seems to figure prominently.

CHAPTER 18

THE HARD PROBLEM

Consciousness or awareness is an important concept in Eastern religions, but it is largely ignored in Western religions. Generally, the Western worldview is based on "materialism," which says that consciousness originates from energy and matter.

Some believe that as the Universe evolves, we develop consciousness. According to philosopher David Chalmers, the "hard problem" of consciousness is the question of how something material, like an organism, could produce something immaterial, like a thought.

The other way of looking at the world, which is more common in the Eastern worldview, is "idealism," which says that energy and matter originate from consciousness, not vice versa. This view makes less sense to some of us, until we recall that solid objects are not really "solid" and that we experience all of our senses in our brains.

Sir James Jeans, an astrophysicist, once wrote, "The universe begins to look more like a great thought than like a great machine." The movie *The Matrix* illustrates this idea. The other hard problem of consciousness is the question of how something immaterial, like a thought, could produce something material, like an organism.

PANPSYCHISM

Another explanation for the relationship of consciousness to energy and matter is called "panpsychism," which suggests that consciousness is inherent in energy and matter. One scientist wryly commented that every academic who studies consciousness eventually either "becomes a panpsychist or goes into administration."

Winston Churchill once suggested that democracy is the worst form of government–except for all the others. Similarly, panpsychism has been described as the worst explanation of consciousness—except for all the others.

Many panpsychists believe that every person or thing—humans, animals, plants, and minerals—has some level of consciousness, relative to its complexity. Biologists have shown that cells can send information to other cells, that plants can send information to other plants, and that animals can send information to other animals.

Is a person more conscious than a rock? A Zen master might ask, "Is a bucket more full than a thimble?" Each is endowed according to its capacity.

If we accept panpsychism, then we have to ask whether consciousness is physical (meaning that it can be explained by biology, chemistry, and physics) or whether consciousness is metaphysical (meaning that it cannot be explained by biology, chemistry, and physics).

PHYSICAL AND
METAPHYSICAL

If consciousness is physical, not metaphysical, and if the big questions, including "How did the Universe begin?" and "How did life begin?" and "How did consciousness arise?" can be explained by biology, chemistry, and physics, then are we all pantheists, who believe that "God" and "the Universe" are the same?

If consciousness is metaphysical, not physical, and if the big questions cannot be explained by the physical sciences, then are we all panentheists, who believe that God interpenetrates the Universe and extends beyond space and time?

If there is a metaphysical world, as well as a physical world, are God and consciousness the same? Do the metaphysical and physical worlds function the same way?

It is tempting to say that the physical world is similar to the metaphysical world ("as above, so below") and that there are parallels between physical concepts and metaphysical concepts, but we can admit that there are parallels without insisting that God has anything to say about physics or that physics has anything to say about God.

Cosmologist Brian Swimme and others suggest that the basic dynamism of the universe is attraction, which manifests as gravity in a physical sense and as love in a metaphysical sense.

If God is the "ground of being," (as philosopher Paul Tillich said) rather than a being, then we might agree that the Universe has order, but can an impersonal Universe have intention?

In other words, is the Universe moving toward complexity and diversity and interconnectedness because God designed it that way or because the Universe evolved that way?

Perhaps the complexity and diversity that we see is the Way of the Universe (how things occur naturally) rather than the Will of God (how God causes them to occur intentionally). Of course, it is also possible that God has intention, but that he chooses not to interfere with the universe.

These are all interesting questions, we cannot know the answers to any of them, and we probably would not live our lives any differently if we did know the answers.

BRAIN AND MIND

Some believe that we share an Akashic record or sacred archive, where the Universe records all of our actions and thoughts. They distinguish between "brains," which are personal to each organism, and "mind," which might be common to all organisms.

In this scenario, the brain is more of a receiver than a transmitter. The left brain, which is considered to be the analytical part of the brain, may actually serve as a filter that focuses the right brain, which is considered to be the intuitive part of the brain.

Without this filter, perhaps we would be unable to function, distracted by every blade of grass and drop of dew.

Neurosurgeon Eben Alexander explains:

> In filter theory, the physical brain serves as the reducing valve or filter through which universal consciousness or the Collective Mind, is filtered, or allowed in, to our more restricted human perception of the world around us.

Dr. Jill Bolte Taylor, a neuroscientist, wrote an interesting book called *A Stroke of Insight,* describing a stroke that she experienced in her left brain, which removed her filters, inhibited her ability to function, and opened her to a mystical experience.

AKASHIC RECORD

When we realize that the Universe is a field and that consciousness occupies this physical or metaphysical field, then we see that our actions and thoughts are connected to others' actions and thoughts.

Various spiritual traditions believe that the Universe records all of our actions and thoughts. Indigenous people talk about a sacred archive. The Vedas talk about the Jewel Net of Indra, in which the Universe is a net of jewels, and each individual jewel reflects the Universe in its totality. The Vedas also talk about an Akashic record, which author Ervin Laszlo has written much about in modern times.

An Akashic record or sacred archive is a non-physical record of human actions, thoughts, and words. Biologists talk about auras and energies that surround organisms, and physicists talk about holograms, where parts of the Universe reflect the whole. Akashic records are consistent with the notion of nonlocality.

Some say that the Universe is configured like a great computer system, where information is stored in an archive, analogous to the cloud. This information can be accessed by our brains, analogous to computers. Our brains can upload information to the archive or download information from the archive. Some programs are executed in the archive, and some programs are executed in our brains.

Also, it is possible that the presence of an Akashic record or sacred archive might explain para-psychological phenomenon, such as extra-sensory perception, near-death experiences, out-of-body experiences, and past-life recollections. If there is no archive, then we do not have any simpler explanation for these unusual occurrences.

How else can we explain what psychologist Carl Jung called the collective unconscious or what physicist David Bohm called the implicate order or what biologist Rupert Sheldrake calls morphic resonance? Is it more likely that collective memory is contained in our genes or embedded in our conditioning, or that there is some type of Akashic record or sacred archive?

Imagine that someone recalling a past life is actually accessing an Akashic record or sacred archive that contains information about a past life. This past life might not necessarily be their personal life; it might be someone else's personal life or our one collective, impersonal life.

CHAPTER 19

AMERICA AT A CROSSROADS

Our nation is at a crossroads. During our lifetimes, our influence has declined steadily, and this is consistent with the lessons of history:

> In the 1700s, France had the world's largest economy.
>
> In the 1800s, Great Britain had the world's largest economy.
>
> In the 1900s, the United States had the world's largest economy.
>
> In the 2000s, China will likely have the world's largest economy.
>
> In the 2100s, India may have the world's largest economy.

Some of the tensions in our culture arise from our waning influence as a nation. Due to environmental degradation and population growth, our planet is struggling, and our resources are stretched, so that we can only have more prosperity if others have less.

Also, our children might not enjoy the prosperity in the future that we enjoy today. Scientists estimate that we may have already reached the point where the planet cannot provide a middle-class living for all of us. Our pie is not growing; our world is zero-sum.

As we realize that the largest economies in the world will soon be China and India, we can expect that Eastern culture, including Eastern religions, will rise in influence, while Western culture, including Western religions, will decline.

THE FOURTH TURNING

Neil Howe and William Strauss developed a theory called the Fourth Turning, which suggests that history follows 80-year cycles, similar in length to a long human life. The Revolutionary War was approximately 80 years before the Civil War, which was approximately 80 years before World War II, which was approximately 80 years ago.

Midway between these low points in the cycle, there are high points in the cycle. For example, approximately 40 years ago, the 1970s were a time of societal change, with the civil rights movement, the environmental movement, and the women's movement.

As I understand the Fourth Turning, we are at a critical inflection point now, and we are entering a period of momentous change and startling possibilities for our society.

In *The Future of Faith,* theologian Harvey Cox writes that we spent 400 years in the Age of Faith, then 1,600 years in the Age of Belief, before entering the Age of the Spirit, which is challenging the old fundamental, hierarchical, patriarchal institutions.

Hopefully, we will find a new spirituality—beyond speculative doctrine, supernatural claims, and unkind practices—that better agrees with the Eastern religions, the mystics, and the scientists.

THE WAY FORWARD

We must choose between our current ideology of personal responsibility and our current theology of personal salvation—and a new ideology of communal responsibility and a new theology of communal salvation.

The Eastern religions, the mystics, and the scientists tell us that our world is much more complex, diverse, and interconnected than we ever realized, whether by design or by evolution. They agree that it is possible that self is a construct, soul is a fallacy, and free will is an illusion.

Much of the doctrine of contemporary Christianity has been discredited in the last few hundred years, and people are less likely to believe in global floods, talking snakes, and virgin birth than they were 100 years ago.

More important, Jesus has a lot to teach us about how to live, and his story is pretty compelling—whether he was actually born of a virgin, whether he actually died for our sins, or whether he was actually physically resurrected.

Many of our lives are transactional. Christianity is transactional too, promising punishment or reward for our bad or good behavior. Theologian John D. Caputo writes:

> Life is a gift we did not ask for. That is the condition of a pure gift, of an unconditional gift—no Infinite Debt, no Big Benefactor in the sky, no choirs of courtiers singing eternal hosannas to the emperor, no rewards and punishments. Just a gift, without why.

Theology has teeth, and it informs our choices. If we realize that God is in everyone and everything, then we would never ban Muslims or build walls or separate families, and we would always want to ensure that everyone has access to food, clothing, and shelter, as well as to child care, education, and health care.

There is an arrogance in Western civilization, particularly in the United States, where we think that we have the answers, that our ideology is exceptional, and that our theology is correct—even though our answers are specific to our culture, our capitalistic ideology is an experiment (which has produced considerable environmental degradation and extreme inequality), and our Western theology is speculation, which does not always agree with reason or science.

THE PERENNIAL PHILOSOPHY

The perennial philosophy of author Aldous Huxley and others, is absolute, authentic, original, rational, unchanging, and universal.

We see that the Eastern religions believe that the Universe is characterized by nonduality, not duality.

We see that the mystics experience a sense of unity, rather than separation. God is immanent and transcendent, God is personal and impersonal, and God is in everyone and everything.

We see that the scientists observe that the universe is a connected field, rather than a collection of discrete objects. Our world is more communal or societal, than individual or personal.

We see that the psychologists believe that mature human development involves transcendence, not actualization, and that mature spiritual development involves universalizing of justice and mercy, not correctness of authority or doctrine.

Author Evelyn Underhill wrote *Mysticism,* the definitive book on mysticism, more than 100 years ago. In it, she wrote:

> The world of religion is no longer a concrete fact proposed for our acceptance and adoration. It is an unfathomable universe which engulfs us, and which lives its own majestic uncomprehended life, and we discover that our careful maps and cherished definitions bear little relation to its unmeasured reality.

Although the Eastern religions, the mystics, and the scientists seem to agree, these common perspectives are in conflict with the dualistic, Newtonian, Western worldview that has characterized contemporary Christian beliefs for the last 1,700 years.

Contrast Christianity with any modern set of practices or system of beliefs. Imagine that the thought leaders in any other art or science or profession decreed that there could be no amendment to the theories that were developed in AD 325, despite all that we have learned in the intervening years.

Rather than engage in speculation about whether God exists or whether Jesus is divine, the Eastern religions, the mystics, and the scientists see the Universe as it is, focus on the here and now (not the afterlife), and seek to transcend the individual, egoic self and to reveal the universal, True Self, by removing filters to glimpse the mind beyond the brain.

Once we grasp the perennial philosophy and the notion that the Universe is characterized by nonduality, not duality, we will encounter it everywhere—in philosophy, psychology, and theology, as well as in biology, chemistry, and physics.

Philosopher Julien Musolino talks about the freedom that comes from abandoning the "soul fallacy" and focusing on the here and now, rather than the afterlife, and on oneness, rather than the self:

> The realization that our days are numbered compels us to try to live in the present. Renewed focus on the here and now also encourages us to develop gratitude. It is often said that happiness is not having what you want but wanting what you have. The conclusion that we are creatures of flesh and blood frees us from the burden of obsessing about the fate of our souls, and inhibiting our selfish impulses allows us to be mindful of the plight of others.... The new worldview that replaces the old one is better and wiser.

Fortunately, you do not have to take my word for it. You can read David Bohm or Joseph Campbell or Mircea Eliade or Albert Einstein or Thich Nhat Hahn or Aldous Huxley or Carl Jung or Abraham Maslow or Plato or Shankara or Baruch Spinoza or Paul Tillich. Many of the great minds in the arts and sciences realize our oneness.

11/9

On November 9, 2016, Donald J. Trump was elected President of the United States. For me, the election was such a shock to the system that I stopped writing for a few years. When I resumed writing, I realized that my last words were written on November 9.

Imagine that you are writing a book about the Eastern religions, the mystics, and the scientists. You realize that everyone is related, and everything is connected. Then, the American people elect Donald Trump, who is seen by many people as a crude, dishonest, greedy, misogynistic, narcissistic, racist, transphobic, xenophobic person.

Soon, he starts banning Muslims and building walls and separating families, as well as attacking our institutions, including Congress, the Courts, and the press. Ultimately, he foments an attack on the Capitol and an insurrection against the government.

TRUMPISM

I suspect that Donald Trump will be disgraced, finally held accountable for his bad behavior in business, in government, and in his personal life. This is already happening.

Many people who consider themselves good Americans, good Christians, and good people supported some terribly un-American, un-Christian, and uncivil actions and ideas.

He was elected once, almost twice, and his support came from "religious" people. Trump was the most public candidate who ever ran for office, and those who supported him knew what they were getting.

Trumpism, which can be characterized by a blatant disregard for others—including immigrants, the disabled, poor, sick, and unemployed—now seems larger and more long-lived than Trump himself.

When so many religious people support such irreligious behavior, then perhaps we need to examine contemporary Christian theology. Theology has teeth, and bad theology breeds bad behavior.

CHURCH AND SOCIETY

Where did we learn to confuse beliefs with facts? We learned that in church. Where did we learn to support people who share our beliefs and to oppose those who do not? We learned that in church.

Where did we learn that God rewards us for our beliefs—and therefore, that God will punish others for theirs? We learned that in church, too.

Author John Pavlovitz explains the danger of overly individualistic thinking:

> Poised on either side of the debate in matters of education and health care and faith and immigration aren't people who love their children and people who don't—but people who love all children and those who care only for their own. We need to love wider and further.

CHAPTER 20

CHRISTIANITY AT A CROSSROADS

JESUS 2.0

Jesus lived in the Middle East, at the confluence of the Eastern and Western worlds, and we largely interpret Jesus through the lens of 2,000 years of Western civilization, without realizing how many of his actions and words reflect nonduality, not duality.

Can one follow Jesus without following Aristotle and Augustine and Anselm? Absolutely. Jesus' words and works do not conflict with the Eastern worldview; in fact, many of Jesus' words and works reflect the Eastern worldview.

For instance, Jesus said that the Kingdom of God is within and that the Kingdom is all around, but we do not see it. The Kingdom is here, and the Kingdom is coming in the future. Jesus did not say that the Kingdom is the church or that the Kingdom is in heaven.

Jesus said that we should pray to the Father and that no one is good but the Father, and he said that his disciples are his friends who should relate to the Father as Jesus does.

In the Gospel of John, Jesus actually said, "You are Gods, sons of the Most High, all of you." Jesus did not say that he is the second person of the Trinity or that he has a different relationship to the Father from anyone else.

Author John Middleton Murry saw Jesus in a modern light:

Jesus believed he was the son of God, in precisely the same sense as he believed all men to be sons of God. The difference between him and other men was simply that he knew he was the son of God, while they did not.

Jesus said that we should live in the here and now and that we should sell our belongings and follow him. Jesus did not say that we should confess our sins to a priest or that we should profess Jesus as our Lord and Savior.

JOHN 14:6

Some Christians point to passages in the Gospel of John, which is a later gospel, to say that there is something exclusive about Jesus.

When Jesus says, "I am the way, and the truth, and the life. No one comes to the Father except through me," he is likely saying that he and the Father are of the same mind, not that they are of the same substance.

Of course, Jesus' way is the way to the Father. As we have said elsewhere, Jesus' way is similar to Buddha's way, to Krishna's way, to Lao Tzu's way, to Muhammed's way, because they, too, are likely of the same mind as God, whom Jesus calls the Father.

In *Theology Without Walls,* philosopher Jerry L. Martin writes, "Perhaps the Jesus who says, 'I am the way, the truth, and the life; no one comes to the Father but through me' is the same 'I' who, as Krishna, says, 'In whatever way living beings approach me, thus do I receive them; all paths lead to me.'"

THE MIND OF GOD

Different beliefs will make sense to different people, according to their conditioning. Christianity originated in the Middle East, where East and West meet:

Did Jesus ever talk about detachment or enlightenment or *karma* or *nirvana*? No, not in those terms.

Did Jesus ever talk about grace or original sin or the soul or the Trinity? No, not in those terms.

Jesus was ambiguous about heaven or hell. Although many Christians believe Jesus' purpose was to die for our sins, many other Christians believe that his purpose was to teach us how to live.

Clearly, Jesus was a remarkable man, a healer, a mystic, and a teacher, on the same level as any remarkable man in any tradition. There are books of "parallel sayings" that demonstrate the similarities between his teachings and those of Buddha and Lao Tzu, just as there are similarities between the Old Testament and the scriptures of other traditions.

However, Jesus' teachings (and the Old Testament writings) are so similar to contemporaneous sacred or secular teachings of other traditions that there is no reason to think that one was written (or inspired) by God and that the others were only written by humans.

If Jesus was God or if the Bible was God's word, it seems to me that these teachings would be superior in all respects to the teachings of other fallible, human traditions.

THE PERSON OF JESUS

Jesus was either a) a wise man or b) a wise man who shared the mind of God or c) a wise man who ultimately became God or d) a deity who was always God.

We cannot know who Jesus thought he was or who his followers thought he was, or whether he or his followers were mistaken in their beliefs. More to the point, it makes no difference, unless we think that God really cares what each of the eight billion of us believe.

Regardless, in an allegorical, metaphorical, or mythical sense, Jesus' story is a beautiful and enlightening one. In fact, it can be a more beautiful and enlightening story when understood allegorically, metaphorically, or mythically, rather than literally.

If Jesus is an example, rather than an exception, then we are all Sons of God, we are all one with the Father, we can all die to self, we can all realize the Kingdom of God, and we can all have eternal life.

Of course, if we experience eternal life in the Eastern sense, rather than the Western sense, then we merge into the impersonal cosmic soup, rather than maintain an individual identity as a person or a soul.

CHRISTIANITY 2.0

Ultimately, I am not trying to argue any specific beliefs or to convince you of anything, as ultimately you have to decide for yourself. However, it seems to me that Christianity has a lot to learn from the other spiritual traditions:

Christianity could acknowledge mysticism, which would require that we seek a direct experience of God. As Catholic theologian Karl Rahner famously wrote, "The Christian of the future will be a mystic or he will not exist at all."

Christianity could become comfortable with paradox and embrace the mystery, which would require that we hold doctrines loosely and pursue experiences of God, rather than speculations about God.

Christianity could recognize advances in history, philosophy, and science, which would require that we rethink some of our ancient beliefs and practices.

In coming years, we can no longer expect modern Christians to believe in global floods, talking snakes, and virgin births, just as (eventually) our forefathers no longer believed that the sun revolved around the earth.

Many Christian realize that their religion is asking them to believe some unbelievable things. Certainly, an omnipotent God can do anything, but God has not done unbelievable things for years, if God has ever done them.

Imagine that Christianity was less doctrinal, more paradoxical, and more respectful of science. In *Hoping Against Hope*, theologian John D. Caputo argues that, increasingly, Christian doctrine is incredible and Christian believers are incredulous. He writes:

The conservatives confirm that religion requires believing fantasies. The progressives confirm that living well has little or nothing to do with believing in religion's supernatural beings and codified doctrines. Indeed, far from being sustained by such beliefs, living well is actually impeded by it and too often results in leading furiously reactionary, intolerant, exclusionary, avaricious, mean-spirited, science-denying and anti-modern lives.

CONCLUSION

EVERYONE IS RELATED,
AND EVERYTHING IS CONNECTED

Throughout this book, I have made a concession to Western readers by repeatedly saying that "Everyone is related, and everything is connected," as if there are many persons and many things.

Ultimately, it seems to me that there is only one person, and he is not a person, and there is only one thing, and it is not a thing. Is this view mystical and paradoxical, yet still respectful of science? Absolutely.

When we say anything more than "The Universe is" or "I Am," then we "collapse the wave function," as the quantum physicists say. In insisting that Schrödinger's cat is either alive or dead, we eliminate the possibility that it is "both alive and dead."

In a black-and-white Newtonian world, there is no paradox, but in a Technicolor quantum Universe, there are paradoxes all around us.

I have given you some food for thought, by challenging my beliefs, posing some interesting questions, and providing some insightful perspectives. Hopefully, you learned something, and you unlearned something too.

Sadly, we will never know whether God exists or whether God is a person or whether the Universe has intention or whether we have selves or souls or free will.

Regardless, I have found that I live a better life when I live as if there is a Oneness, as if we are supposed to bring our understanding of the absolute world, which is Oneness, to our relative world, which can seem disconnected and divided.

Gesshin Claire Greenwood, a Zen nun, reflects on the Oneness, the "embeddedness":

> We receive life from the universe. Usually, we think that we are in charge of our breathing and digestion, but this is actually happening without our consciousness. We receive our life, we borrow this life, an infinite number of organisms support us in living. Once we notice this embeddedness, we feel compelled to act and face the world from a place of gratitude and responsibility—to work and study deeply, to practice in every moment, to smile, to own our own anger and jealousy, to not waste time. No one else can do this for us, and there is no time to do it but the present moment.

The more we understand God, the more we understand ourselves. Further, the more we understand ourselves, the more we transform ourselves, our families, our communities, and our world. Dr. Martin Luther King, Jr. said this in a Christmas sermon:

> It really boils down to this: that all life is interrelated. We are all caught in an inescapable network of mutuality, tied in a single garment of destiny. Whatever affects one directly, affects all indirectly. We are made to live together because of the interrelated structure of reality.

Author Yanhao Huang reminds us of the actionless action of the Taoists when he writes, "If you realize that everything in existence is fundamentally you, then you will not need to be taught to be kind to others, to care for the environment, to end violence, and so on. You will do them effortlessly because it's in your nature to do so."

I hope that you see how the Eastern religions, the mystics, and the scientists suggest that everyone is related, and everything is connected. When you get that point, and when it changes you and your spiritual practice, then your belief system is secondary.

As long as you can blow new life into them, you can even keep your old bones.

The Journey Is the Destination

One day, my wife and I watched old home movies with our son and daughter and son-in-law. The camera panned around a house that we no longer own, in a neighborhood where we no longer live, filled with possessions that we no longer have, and rested on some beloved relatives and some cherished pets who are no longer with us.

The camera found my pretty wife of seven years and my sweet children, ages five and two. Soon, it found me, a 29-year-old man at the beginning of a 25-year career in investment banking. *So, that's how I looked before I gained 50 pounds and lost a million dollars,* I thought.

Then, I missed my in-laws and my dog and my house and my neighborhood and my stuff, and I missed my pretty wife and my sweet children, and I missed my strong, young self.

"I am as old now as you were then," my daughter said wistfully.

I leaned into the TV, intently staring at my 29-year-old self, as he leaned into the camera, intently staring at me, or so it seemed.

Suddenly, I felt the piercing gaze of my 29-year-old self, as he scanned my surroundings. He saw my house and my neighborhood and my stuff, and he saw my wife of 32 years and my children, now aged 29 and 26. He saw my son-in-law, soon to be a father himself.

Somehow, he knew that my life had worked out well. He knew that I had lost the 50 pounds and recovered the million dollars, just as he knew that we were retired, that we were healthy, and that our children were established.

He knew that I spent my time driving veterans to the VA clinic and helping people with their taxes and playing with sick children at a children's hospital and teaching writing at a library and volunteering for the Red Cross. *A good life,* he thought. *No, a great life.*

Then he wanted my life and my pretty wife and my successful children and my old, steady self—and I knew that he would, since he was always in a hurry to find the future.

"Hug your in-laws, kiss your wife, love your kids, play with your dog," I said to my young self. "You are in a hurry. Savor the moment. Take your time. The journey is the destination."

He nodded silently, as the camera panned away slowly.

Suggestions for Further Reading

The Power of Myth by Joseph Campbell (or anything by Joseph Campbell) is a great place to start. The book is a transcript of interviews of Campbell, one of the greatest thinkers of the last century, by Bill Moyers, one of the greatest interviewers of the last century. Campbell recognizes the powerful symbols that appear in many traditions.

The Bhagavad Gita translated by Eknath Easwaran is a classic Vedic scripture that recounts a conversation between a warrior, Arjuna, and his spiritual guide, Krishna, who appears in the form of Arjuna's charioteer. There is no better introduction to Eastern religions.

Tao Te Ching by Lao Tzu is a classic Taoist text. The Tao or the Way describes the essential force of the Universe. Before I read the mystics, I could not understand how God could be perceived as a force or a presence, rather than a person, in the East. After I studied the mystics, the Eastern religions, and the scientists, I understood it.

The Heart of the Buddha's Teaching by Thich Nhat Hanh (or anything by Thich Nhat Hanh) is a good introduction to Buddhist thought. Buddhism is seen as a way of life, rather than a religion, and it is concerned with right behavior, rather than right belief. Christianity began this way, too, until the priests and the theologians took over.

Jesus in the Lotus by Russill Paul (or anything by Bede Griffiths) describes the time that Paul spent with Bede Griffiths, who lived simultaneously as a Christian mystic and as a Hindu holy man at an ashram in India. Griffiths honored both traditions, without compromising either.

Without Buddha, I Could Not Be a Christian by Paul F. Knitter describes the journey of a former Catholic priest who explored Buddhism and reevaluated his Christian doctrine in the light of his Buddhism. Today, Knitter is a Christian and a Buddhist, who has attained deeper understanding of his Christian faith through Buddhist insights.

Meister Eckhart by Meister Eckhart and Bernard McGinn (editor) contains the writings of one of the great Christian mystics. Eckhart was a proponent of the "via negativa" or the path of negation, believing that language is inadequate to describe God. (*Neti Neti*, as the Hindus say, meaning "Not this, not that.")

The Cloud of Unknowing by (appropriately) Anonymous is a spiritual guide to contemplative prayer that urges its readers to seek experience of God, rather than knowledge of God. The practice of centering prayer was inspired by this book.

The Dark Night of the Soul by John of the Cross is the best-known work by the best-known Christian mystic. The book describes the spiritual journey and the dark night that the journey often entails.

(Although both are revered today, Meister Eckhart was tried for heresy and John of the Cross was tortured by his brother monks. Perhaps that is why the author of *The Cloud* remained anonymous!)

Contemplation by Willigis Jäger is the best book on the practice of Christian contemplation. Jäger is a Benedictine monk and a Zen master, so he writes from a Christian perspective, but he understands the Eastern perspective too.

Tales of the Hasidim by Martin Buber is an example of the Jewish wisdom tradition. The Hasidic rabbis were influential wisdom teachers in the 1700s and 1800s.

The Desert Fathers by Benedicta Ward (editor) is an example of the Christian wisdom tradition. The desert fathers were monastics who lived in the deserts of Egypt, Palestine, and Syria in the 400s.

Tales of the Dervishes by Idries Shah (or anything by Idries Shah) is an example of the Muslim wisdom tradition. Shah released several collections of Sufi stories, which are often humorous and always insightful.

The Way of Chuang Tzu by Thomas Merton (or anything by Thomas Merton) is an example of the Taoist wisdom tradition. Merton was a twentieth century Christian mystic who studied Eastern religions.

The Essential Rumi by Jalal al-Din Rumi and Coleman Barks is a collection of poetry by a thirteenth century Sufi mystic. Rumi is the most popular poet in the United States. His poetry is enigmatic, but a list like this would not be complete without it.

Celebration of Discipline by Richard J. Foster is a guide to Christian spirituality, consisting of twelve inward, outward, and corporate disciplines, such as prayer and fasting. Foster is a Quaker, and his spirituality is more mystical than doctrinal.

In the Spirit of Happiness by the Monks of New Skete has been described as "a monastic retreat in book form." Often, I give this book to friends, because it is so practical. The monks breed and train dogs, and they publish excellent books on dog training.

Christianity by Hans Küng is the only 900-page book on the list. It traces the development of Christianity from the first century to the twenty first century, describing how doctrines such as the Trinity, the divinity of Jesus, the primacy of the pope, and the justification by faith took mainstream Christianity farther and farther from its early Jewish Christian roots.

Saving Jesus from the Church by Robin R. Meyers is an insightful book that really resonated with me after studying philosophy, theology, and spirituality for over 20 years. This is a relevant and timely book that attempts to reclaim the legacy of Jesus and the spirit of early Christianity.

Food for the Heart by Ajahn Chah helped me to understand the Buddhist perspective on suffering. Because this is such a practical book, it was much more compelling to me than many of the more philosophical books on the same subject, and it really opened the door to Eastern religions for me.

Be As You Are by Ramana Maharshi explains the practice of self-inquiry, which focuses on the question "Who Am I?" The practice is designed to strip away the egoic self, leaving only the authentic Self or "I Am." Ramana Maharshi was the real deal.

Christ the Guru by Swami Muni Narayana Prasad and *The Zen Teachings of Jesus* by Kenneth S. Leong are two books that examine Christianity from an Eastern perspective. They show that Jesus' message is universal and that it has been subsumed by Christian theology (Augustine, Aquinas, Anselm) and Greek philosophy (Aristotle, Plato). Can we follow Jesus without following Aristotle or Augustine?

History of Mysticism by Swami Abhayananda is a survey of the major mystical traditions and their understandings of God. The author identifies two consistent themes, which correspond to Ramakrishna's notions of "God with name and form" (a personal god) and "God without name and form" (an impersonal or transpersonal god).

The Tao of Physics by Fritjof Capra explores the parallels between modern physics and Eastern mysticism. The science is interesting and the spirituality is interesting, but the parallels are REALLY interesting. This is a good introduction for someone who does not want to read every physics book on the shelf.

The Courage to Be by Paul Tillich (or anything by Paul Tillich) is a classic by the renowned Christian philosopher. Tillich has a broader perspective than most Christian philosophers, and his concept of God as the "ground of being" is universal.

The Farther Reaches of Human Nature by Abraham H. Maslow is an expansion of his well-known work on self-actualization. In this posthumous work, Maslow discusses the concept of transcendence. The self is a critical concept in spirituality, and Maslow suggests that the final step in realizing our selves is to transcend our selves.

The Ego Trick by Julian Baggini is a deconstruction of the elusive concept of the self. Baggini concludes that the self is a bundle of associations, ephemeral and fluid, and that the self is not identical to our bodies and brains or our personalities and thoughts. What does that tell us about our ourselves and our gods?

Conscious by Annaka Harris is a short but compelling book about consciousness, in which the author explores consciousness, free will, and the self. She examines the "hard problem" of philosophy—how matter produces consciousness—by suggesting panpsychism (that consciousness is inherent in matter) as a viable theory.

Healing Breath by Ruben L.F. Habito is a clear and compelling description of Zen practice, which is written from a Christian perspective by a former Jesuit priest. In the book, Habito suggests that Christian beliefs are compatible with Zen practices.

SUGGESTIONS FOR STUDY QUESTIONS

A few years ago, my adult children asked incredulously "What happened to you? You used to be a conservative, Catholic, Republican, investment banker. Now, you are an open-hearted and open-minded person. You cry more, and you laugh more. You live a life of connection and reflection and service. What happened to you?"

Well, I read 1,000 books, then I baked in a sweat lodge, chanted to Shiva, meditated in a zendo, and whirled with the dervishes. I deconstructed everything about my old conventional, Christian belief system and reconstructed a new, unconventional belief system—based on the Eastern religions, the mystics, and the scientists—where everyone is related, and everything is connected.

Honestly, if I had to explain it all, I would have to write a book about it. "You need to write that book!" they exclaimed. So, I did.

THE BOOK

The book concludes that "Everyone is related, and everything is connected." This statement seems to me to be the most defensible and least damaging creed that anyone could adopt. Further, it is much more practical and profound than anything that I learned in 50 years of listening to homilies.

Some astute readers describe my path as "Christian, but not too Christian" or "Zen, but not too Zen." I hope that the book can help readers to find their paths, either inside or outside of organized religion. Also, I hope that readers will explore perspectives outside of their native traditions.

The book is conversational. When I wrote the book, I barely had any record of my journey, so I worked from memory, as if I were having a casual discussion. Looking back, I think that my lack of preparation helped me to write a better book.

The book is inclusive. Many readers appreciate that the book leaves room for other beliefs (or no beliefs). Some people do not respect my views, but I respect theirs, and I do not pass judgment.

The book is personal. The book was modeled on the "ethical will" from the Jewish tradition. An ethical will is NOT an autobiography. Instead, an ethical will is written to communicate one's experiences, life lessons, and values.

The book is reporting. My intent was to tell only as much of my smaller, more personal story as was necessary to serve the larger, more universal story.

The book is serious. The subject matter is serious, and some people can misinterpret questions about religion to be cynical or dismissive or irreverent.

The book is unconventional. The first part examines Christian orthodoxy, without being angry or judgmental, and the second part integrates a modern spirituality—based on the Eastern religions, the mystics, and the scientists—without being preachy or speculative.

HOW TO READ THE BOOK

When we discuss the book at author talks and book clubs, it generates plenty of discussion. The material is interesting, the presentation is clear and fair, and the questions are open-ended.

Often, it is enough to step through the book, asking, "What did you learn? What did you like or dislike? Did anything challenge you? Did anything resonate with you?"

At the end of several chapters, the book asks readers to "Imagine that…" These thought experiments challenge readers to "riff" on the content, and they generate some good discussions.

COMMUNITY AND PRACTICE

One in three Americans experience some form of religious trauma, either emotionally, mentally, physically, or sexually.

When I meet someone on a spiritual journey, I will ask them, "Are you angry? What is your community? What is your spiritual practice?" Many are angry, and many do not have a community or a spiritual practice anymore. I hope that the book will encourage readers to release anger and to reclaim community and practice.

For me, church did not work, and religion did not work, but spirituality was transformative, so I do not like to see anyone give up on spirituality because they do not accept the speculative doctrine, supernatural claims, or unkind practices of their native religions.

YOU MIGHT BE RIGHT

In my first author talk, I talked about a good friend who visited us in Crestone. As we discussed the book, he said that he thought that the earth was 6,000 years old and that the dinosaurs died in the global flood.

I replied, "This is just my opinion, but we are at 8,000 feet above sea level. Did the water get here? Where did the water come from? Where did the water go? Why do we NOT find dinosaur bones and human bones in the same locations?"

Then, I said the important part. "You might be right." I was not here 6,000 years ago or 14 billion years ago. "You might be right" has become my mantra, because it begins or ends a conversation gracefully, acknowledging that reasonable people can agree to disagree.

I hope that you enjoy reading *The Way* as much as I enjoyed writing it.

As you read the book,
you might consider the following questions:

INTRODUCTION

1. Did you ever deconstruct or reconstruct your belief system? Did you ever experience a dark night of the soul? Do you have any religious trauma?

2. Have you rejected church or God or religion or spirituality? If so, what is your community, and what is your practice? Do you belong to a church, or do you seek universal Truth in several different places?

3. How would you "blow new life into old bones" in your spiritual life?

BRAHMACHARYA (THE STUDENT)

1. Do you still practice your childhood religion? If so, do you still practice this religion in the same way that you did then? If not, why not?

2. How did your childhood influence your spiritual journey? If you have children, how did your childhood religion impact what you taught your children about religion? Do your children share your beliefs now?

3. Do you need to reclaim or renounce anything from your childhood religion? If you belong to a church, do you share your church's values?

CHAPTER 1: WORLDVIEWS

1. In the East, some think that self is a construct, soul is a fiction, and free will is an illusion, suggesting that we are all living one impersonal life, rather than many personal lives. Would you live your life differently if you adopted an Eastern worldview?

2. In the West, how has our individualistic worldview affected our spirituality? Conversely, how has our individualistic spirituality affected our worldview?

3. If the Universe is eternal, would you believe in a God who is not its creator? If God is the ground of being, then a separation between God and man is impossible, and Jesus' sacrificial death was unnecessary. Would you follow a Jesus who lived an exemplary life, but who did not die for our sins?

CHAPTER 2: GOD

1. What are your beliefs about God? Does God exist? Is God a person? If so, how so? Is God omnipotent, omniscient, omnipresent? Can God change? Does God ever intervene in human affairs? If so, why? If not, why not?

2. How have your beliefs about God changed since childhood? As you mature, does it become more difficult or less difficult to believe in God?

3. How do you answer tough questions about God, such as why God permits evil, why God remains hidden, and why God sends people to hell?

CHAPTER 3: THE GENTILES, PAGANS, AND ROMANS

1. Why did a world religion develop around the teachings of Jesus, rather than the teachings of Apollonius of Tyana?

2. How did Christianity change when a small, tribal religion of pacifism became the official, state religion of the greatest empire in the world? Today, is Christianity a religion of the oppressed or the oppressor?

3. What did first century Christianity look like the day after Jesus died, before there was any Bible, any clergy, or any doctrine? Would Jesus recognize a Catholic Mass, a Pentecostal revival, or a Quaker meeting today?

CHAPTER 4: THE JEWS
AND THE JEWISH CHRISTIANS

1. Have you read any interpretations of the Hebrew Bible by Jewish scholars? Are you surprised that the Jews do NOT see any references to Jesus there or that they do NOT believe that Christians superseded Jews as chosen people?

2. If many Jewish scholars are correct that Adam, Abraham, Moses, and Noah may not have existed or that the exodus or the flood may not have occurred, what would be the impact on contemporary Christian doctrine?

3. Why do Catholics revere Peter, why do Protestants revere Paul, and why do neither of them revere James, who was featured in several Bible accounts and who led the early Jewish Christian community for 30 years?

GRIHASTHA (THE HOUSEHOLDER)

1. Did you neglect your spiritual life when you were pursuing a career and/or raising a family? Did you get caught up in the rat race, maybe unwittingly? What can you do to enliven your spiritual life and overcome the rat race?

2. Did you ever leave a church? Did you ever feel like a church left you? If so, were the friends that you made in church still your friends after you left?

3. When you embraced or rejected religion, did it trouble family and friends? Were you angry then, or are you angry now? How do you deal with your anger? Have you made peace with everyone involved? Is that possible for you?

CHAPTER 5: THE GOSPELS

1. Do you think that the birth narratives, the genealogies, and the post-resurrection appearances, added to the later Gospels, are editorial or historical?

2. Do you think that the more laudatory terms of Jesus, the more poetical descriptions of Jesus, and the more spectacular miracle stories, added to the later Gospels, are editorial or historical?

3. Do you think that the Jews and (later) the Jewish Christians— strict monotheists who were awaiting a kingly messiah—would have accepted a trinitarian God and a peasant messiah who was crucified on a cross?

CHAPTER 6: THE GENTILE CHRISTIANS

1. Do you think that many Christian truth claims would be accepted today, if they had been revealed in a recent archaeological discovery, without the benefit of 2,000 years of enthusiastic and (sometimes) violent evangelization?

2. Does it seem strange that the letter of James was largely ignored, that the letters of Paul said almost nothing about the words and works of Jesus, and that the Didache seemed to suggest a human (not divine) view of Jesus?

3. Would Christianity have been accepted over the last 2,000 years if they knew then what we know now about history, mythology, philosophy, and psychology? Would Christianity have evolved differently if they had known about other religious traditions and modern scientific discoveries?

CHAPTER 7: THE CATHOLICS
AND THE PROTESTANTS

1. Are you surprised that some doctrines serve to support organized religion? Would Catholics hold their beliefs as strongly if they rejected apostolic succession or papal infallibility? Would Protestants hold their beliefs as strongly if they rejected biblical inerrancy or justification by faith?

2. Why is it important for some to worship with those who share their beliefs? Do you agree with every belief that your church espouses? Are you harmed if the person in the next pew does not share your beliefs?

3. Does it require more "faith" to believe in unbelievable things or to trust in a God that you can never hope to understand? How do we demonstrate faith? How do we demonstrate trust? Are we justified by faith?

CHAPTER 8: JESUS

1. Are you surprised that Wikipedia listed three types of Christian values? Do we risk creating Jesus in our own image? Can you think of Bible passages that are read differently by conservative Christians and liberal Christians?

2. Do you think that God is partial or impartial? Were Jews really "chosen," and are Christians really "saved"? Why would God prefer one over another?

3. In Chapter 2, I suggested that if we are following Jesus, we are often following Buddha, Lao Tzu, and Muhammed too. Is Jesus' message unique? How is Jesus different from other spiritual leaders, and how is he similar?

CHAPTER 9: THE CONTEMPORARY CHRISTIANS

1. What are the essential aspects of the person of Jesus? How could we correct or reverse some misunderstandings about his person, particularly those that produce some bad behavior among his contemporary Christian followers?

2. Is a statement of beliefs, like a catechism, creed, or confession, necessary? Are certain beliefs essential to Christianity? What would a contemporary Christian creed look like, if it were to reflect our modern understandings of other religious traditions and of scientific discoveries?

3. Theologian John D. Caputo poses a provocative question, asking, "Does the Kingdom of God need God?" Could we accept the teachings of Jesus without accepting the speculative beliefs, supernatural claims, and unkind doctrines that surround him?

VANAPRASTHA: THE FOREST DWELLER

1. Have you ever had an experience outside of your routine that blessed you with a broader or deeper understanding? Have you ever met a person outside of your circle who blessed you with a newer and richer perspective?

2. Have you ever heard a saying or a story that changed the course of your life, like the story of the rich young man changed the course of my life?

3. Twelve step recovery programs rely on a "Power greater than ourselves." What is the "Power greater than ourselves" in your life? In tough times, where do you draw your strength? Have you ever yielded to that Power, as I did during my epiphany on the street corner in Accra?

CHAPTER 10: THE MYSTICS

1. Have you ever had a mystical experience, as described in this chapter? If so, did you recognize it as a mystical experience? Did it change your life?

2. Do you think that we learn about God or the Universe from the mystics, especially since their experiences are so similar, or do you think that these experiences are anecdotal or unreliable? Are you surprised that these experiences are more consistent with the Eastern worldview?

3. Do you think that our ideas about God or the Universe can be limiting? Buddhists encourage us not to mistake the finger pointing at the moon for the moon itself. Are we too caught up in our concepts to recognize reality?

CHAPTER 11: TRANSCENDENCE

1. Are transcendent experiences prompted by brain stimulations, hallucinogens, seizures, or strokes as "authentic" as those prompted by meditation or prayer? Can we validate any transcendent experience?

2. Do you meditate? Is your practice based on attention, mindfulness, or stillness? How has it helped you? How has it frustrated you?

3. In Eastern religions, "enlightenment" is the realization of Ultimate Reality. Is there an equivalent experience in Western religions? Is the realization of Oneness in the East like the union of Creator and creation in the West?

CHAPTER 12: THE EASTERN RELIGIONS

1. Have you ever considered the non-dual Eastern worldview, where God and humans are not separated, as opposed to the dualistic Western worldview, where God and humans are separated? Does this view make sense to you?

2. In the Western worldview, we perceive the relative world, where people and things are apparently separated. In the Eastern worldview, we perceive that the relative world emerges from an absolute world that lacks separation. Does this view make sense to you?

3. Do you think that actions are moral because God decrees them to be so or because they are inherently moral and God recognizes them to be so? Without absolute moral codes, would we be undone by immoral behavior?

CHAPTER 13: HINDUISM

1. Separation is a recurring theme in Christianity, and lack of separation is a recurring theme in the Eastern religions. Fundamentally, do you believe that the Universe is characterized by Oneness or by separation?

2. Have you ever asked yourself "Who am I?" After you discard the characteristics that are ephemeral and impermanent, what is left? Also, is this "I" that remains the same as what remains of everyone else?

3. There are several female deities in Hinduism. In Christianity, the closest thing to a female deity is Catholic reverence for Mary, the mother of Jesus. Can we reclaim a sense of the divine feminine in the Western worldview? How might the divine feminine rehabilitate Western civilization?

CHAPTER 14: BUDDHISM AND TAOISM

1. Do you think that the Eastern emphasis on reducing suffering suggests a more compassionate approach than the Western emphasis on reducing sin? When we reduce suffering, do we take better care of ourselves and others?

2. Do you think that it is nihilistic to emphasize impermanence, suffering, and no-self, or do you think that it is realistic to emphasize those attributes? Should we place more emphasis on these attributes in Christianity?

3. At this point, you are probably seeing that these Eastern and Western worldviews are at odds with each other. When you reconstruct your beliefs, consider them through Eastern and Western lenses. Which makes sense to you?

SANNYASA (THE RENUNCIANT)

1. Have you ever looked for God or the Universe in another spiritual tradition? If so, who or what did you encounter, and how did that experience compare to your customary experience in your native tradition?

2. At several of the spiritual centers in Crestone, there was a focus on energy, which might be called *chi* or *prana* or *ruah*. Recently, radical theologian Clayton Crockett wrote a book called *Energy and Change*, where he describes energy (like God) as the principle of change. What is energy? What is God? What is the difference between energy and God?

3. The Teyuna named evangelization as the biggest threat to their culture. Consider the damage in the name of colonization, crusades, and holy wars. Do the ends justify the means? Is evangelism harmful or helpful?

CHAPTER 15: THE SCIENTISTS

1. Does it matter to you if God did not create the universe or if Adam was mythical or if Jesus did not die for our sins or if we are not alone in the universe?

2. Singer Tom Waits says that "We are all just monkeys with money and guns." Assuming that there is no "bright line" between animals and humans, would this change how we live our lives or how we think about ourselves?

3. Do you believe in the efficacy of intention or prayer? How would that work? Would God answer our prayers, or would we answer our own prayers?

   Imagine that everyone on earth prayed sincerely to end wars. If we united, could humans achieve something that God has not yet been able to achieve? If so, how do we reconcile that with the image of an omnipotent God?

CHAPTER 16: THE QUANTUM PHYSICISTS

1. The book presents a God that is very different from the bearded old man, using phrases like "architecture of the Universe," "ground of being," and "Luminous Web." Do these descriptions make sense to you?

2. Spiritual teacher Gary Zukav suggests that quantum physics replaces the term "observer" with the term "participator." If we are participators who are connected to everyone and everything around us, rather than observers who are watching what goes on, would this change how we live our lives?

3. The book presents a Universe that is probabilistic, rather than deterministic or random. Photons are particles and waves simultaneously. Schrödinger's Cat is alive and dead until the probability function collapses. Why do Eastern religions accept paradox better than Western religions?

CHAPTER 17: CONSCIOUSNESS

1. Do you think that we have souls? If so, what do they do, and where are they? Do you agree with Julien Musolino that souls are like the emperor's clothes? If we do not have souls, what are the theological implications? Does the possibility that we might NOT have souls disturb you?

2. Do you think that we have free will? If not, or (at least) if we do not have as much free will as we think we have, what are the theological implications? Does the possibility that we might NOT have much free will disturb you?

3. Do you think that transcendence is more developed than self-actualization? Can we transcend our egoic selves if we have not first actualized ourselves? Are psychological counseling and spiritual direction different disciplines?

CHAPTER 18: THE HARD PROBLEM

1. What is a thought? How do we think thoughts? Do thoughts arise from within or from without our bodies and brains? Can we control thoughts?

2. The book suggests a difference between brains, which are personal and physical, and mind, which might be impersonal and metaphysical. What do you think of this mind, sometimes described as an Akashic record or sacred archive?

3. Has this book changed how you think about God, the Universe, or yourself? (Note: the question assumes that there is a "you" who has "thoughts," but maybe you are beginning to question these assumptions.)

CHAPTER 19: AMERICA AT A CROSSROADS

1. Do you think that our society realizes that our global influence is waning and that our resources are stretched to the breaking point? Do you think that we realize that we might be near the low point of an 80-year cycle and that our history suggests that there might be better days ahead?

2. Do you think that our society could ever embrace the perennial philosophy? Would we be less likely to ban Muslims, build walls, marginalize LGBTQ people, or separate families, if we recognized our Oneness?

3. Can you envision a world that is more aware of Oneness, where spirituality informs our politics and where political and religious beliefs are disentangled? What can we do to minimize religiously-sanctioned prejudice?

CHAPTER 20: CHRISTIANITY AT A CROSSROADS

1. Christianity has forced us to believe many unbelievable things, and Christianity has doubled down on some of the most unbelievable doctrines. Can Christianity change? What happens to Christianity if it cannot change?

2. John 14:6 is a unique passage that exerts a disproportionate influence. Earlier in the book, I suggested that John likely added material, not that Matthew, Mark, and Luke omitted material. Which do you believe?

3. Do you think that an allegorical, metaphorical, or mythical understanding (as opposed to a literal understanding) of the Bible adds to or subtracts from the power of Jesus' message? Does Jesus' message hold up either way?

CONCLUSION

1. In this chapter, I say that "There is only one person, and he is not a person, and there is only one thing, and it is not a thing." What is God (or the Universe) if he (or it) is not a person (or a thing)?

2. Some readers might think that my one-line creed is overly simplistic, but can we go far wrong if we simply love our neighbors as ourselves and recognize our interconnectedness?

3. Did you blow new life into your old bones? Did you keep your old bones? Has this book challenged you to deconstruct or reconstruct your beliefs?

ACKNOWLEDGEMENTS

As a seeker and a writer, I am grateful to so many people for their insight, encouragement, and criticism.

Jill Jordan, my wife, is my partner on this journey. Although we are different people than we were when we met 50 years ago, we have grown closer, and we have shared an amazing life. On my best days, I am almost as open-hearted and open-minded as Jill. She inspires me.

Lauren Orozco and Marc Jordan, our children, are my most enthusiastic cheerleaders and my most insightful critics. On my best days, I am not as kind nor as wise as either of them. They teach me a lot.

Bear Orozco, our son-in-law, and Meaghan Jordan, our daughter-in-law, offered advice and support, and Ken and Pat Jordan, my dad and mom, and my extended family also offered advice and support.

Chad Maples was a young man who introduced me to Eastern religions. Chad passed away tragically. Always, I will remember him as a cool brother, a good friend, a loving son, and a wise mentor.

William Howell introduced us to the Camino de Crestone and the community of Crestone, Colorado. William is a seeker and a writer, and he has been a dear friend and a valuable mentor to me.

James O'Dea is an activist and a mystic, who challenged me to blow new life into old bones.

The community of Crestone, Colorado, in general, and the numerous spiritual centers there, in particular, have been our "home away from home" for several years, especially Golden Light Sufi Circle, Haidakhandi Universal Ashram, Karma Thegsum Tashi Gomang, Shumei International Institute, The Spiritual Life Institute, and The Way of Nature, to name a few.

Several physical and virtual communities provided nourishment and refuge during my journey, including Arlington Unitarian

Universalist Church and the Meaning of Life group, Susan Scott and the Center for Non-Religious Spirituality, Chalice Abbey and the Deep Dialogue group, David Hayward (Naked Pastor) and The Lasting Supper group, Michael Marsh and the Racism discussion group, the Society for Hindu-Christian Studies, the Sons of Abraham, Unity of Arlington and the Tuesday Nights, and Westar Institute.

Several good friends offered insights, refuted bad ideas, supported good ideas, or spent time with us, including Stephen Barry, Emily Coldren, Dennis Elliott, Chuck Fisher, Karl and Laura Forehand, Howard Gilberg, David Hargrave, Kevin Janosky, Larry Lechtenberg, Peter Lynch, Clete McAlister, Dwain May, Wayne Ogle, Andrew Reichert, Brian Paulson, Barbara Salser, Peter Stanley, Tom and Robin Virtue, and Roger Wolsey.

Ruben Habito, Helen Cortes, and the Maria Kannon Zen Center sangha offered shelter from the storm.

Brian Allain at Writing for Your Life offered helpful advice to get me started on the book, Teja Watson offered invaluable editing expertise, and Steve Kuhn offered invaluable design expertise.

Jim Palmer supported the book and wrote the Foreword. When I finished the book, I looked around to see if others had reached some of the same understandings or traversed some of the same territory, and I found Jim Palmer. Jim is a friend, a mentor, and a trailblazer for me and many other spiritual writers.

The book was inspired by our three grandsons—Jase Orozco, Liam Jordan, and Noah Jordan. Mala and Papa love you.

ABOUT THE AUTHOR

Larry Jordan was raised in a conservative, Christian household. His spiritual journey changed his politics and his religion, even his personality. Today, he is a follower of Jesus with a Zen practice.

Larry spent 25 years in investment banking, assisting companies, governments, and non-profit agencies in issuing over $10 billion of municipal bonds for capital projects and cash flow needs, including airports, colleges, hospitals, power plants, sports facilities, and toll bridges.

In 2011, realizing that his karma bank was overdrawn, Larry left his big job and sold his beautiful house to spend his life in service. Over the next ten years, he spent one year taking care of his grandson, one month teaching school in Africa, and several weeks as a camp counselor for children with serious illnesses and injuries. Also, he drove hundreds of veterans to the Veterans Administration clinic, participated in the annual homeless count for several years, prepared over 1,000 federal income tax returns for low-income families, and volunteered for the American Red Cross disaster action team.

Over the last 20 years, Larry traveled around the world, read over 1,000 books about spirituality, and had some powerful experiences in several spiritual traditions, including baking in a sweat lodge, chanting to Shiva, meditating in a zendo, and whirling with the dervishes.

Larry and his wife, Jill, have two grown children and three young grandsons. They live in Arlington, Texas and Crestone, Colorado, where Larry wrote this book, and they spend their time meditating, playing with their grandchildren, traveling, and volunteering.

Thank you for your interest in *The Way*.

For comments or questions,
feel free to contact the author at
larryjordanauthor@gmail.com.

Made in the USA
Monee, IL
21 November 2023

47067559R00139